DK EYEWITNESS

ENCYCLOPEDIA

POSTER BOOK

DK Delhi
Senior Editor Neha Ruth Samuel
Senior Art Editor Vikas Chauhan
Project Editors Shahid Qureshi, Upamanyu Das
Assistant Art Editor Abhimanyu Adhikary
Senior Picture Researcher Deepak Negi
Managing Editor Kingshuk Ghoshal
Managing Art Editor Govind Mittal
DTP Designers Pawan Kumar, Ashok Kumar

DK London
Senior Editor Carron Brown
Project Editor Camilla Hallinan
Art Editor Chrissy Checketts
Managing Editor Francesca Baines
Managing Art Editor Philip Letsu
Production Editor Gillian Reid
Senior Production Controller Sarah Hovell
Jacket Designer Stephanie Cheng Hui Tan
Jacket Editor Vicky Richards
Publisher Andrew Macintyre
Art Director Mabel Chan
Managing Director Sarah Larter

This edition first published in Great Britain in 2024 by Dorling Kindersley Limited
DK, One Embassy Gardens, 8 Viaduct Gardens, London, SW11 7BW

The authorised representative in the EEA is Dorling Kindersley Verlag GmbH. Arnulfstr. 124, 80636 Munich, Germany

Content previously published as wallcharts in *Eyewitness* books: *Dinosaur* (2021), *Cat* (2022), *Horse* (1990, 2003, 2011, 2024), *Fish* (1990, 2005, 2022), *Shark* (2022), *Ocean* (2021), *Amazon* (2015, 2022), *Insect* (2023), *Reptile* (1991, 2002, 2007, 2014, 2023), *Bird* (2007, 2024), *Rock & Mineral* (2021), *Crystal & Gem* (1991, 2002, 2007, 2014, 2023), *Fossil* (2017, 2023), *Volcano & Earthquake* (2022), *Weather* (2022), *Hurricane & Tornado* (2021), *Natural Disasters* (2022), *Wonders of the World* (2014, 2022), *Periodic Table* (2018, 2022), *Planets* (2022), *Human Body* (2015, 2023), *Train* (2022), *Flight* (1990, 2003, 2011, 2024), *Ancient Egypt* (2021), *Ancient Greece* (1992, 2007, 2014, 2023), *Ancient Rome* (2022), *Viking* (1994, 2002, 2010, 2024), *Knight* (2007, 2015, 2024), *Titanic* (2021), *World War I* (1992, 2007, 2014, 2023), *World War II* (2021)

10 9 8 7 6 5 4 3 2 1
001–344951–Nov/2024

A CIP catalogue record for this book is available from the British Library
ISBN: 978-0-2417-1686-1

Printed and bound in China

www.dk.com

This book was made with Forest Stewardship Council™ certified paper – one small step in DK's commitment to a sustainable future.
Learn more at **www.dk.com/uk/information/sustainability**

The publisher would like to thank the following people for their help with making the book:
Rupa Rao and Vicky Richards for editorial assistance; Prateek Maurya and Beth Johnston for design assistance; Rashika Kachroo for jacket finishes; Deepak Mittal for DTP assistance; and Ridhima Sikka and Samrajkumar S for help with picture research.

The publisher would like to thank the following for their kind permission to reproduce their images:
(a=above; b=below/bottom; c=centre; f=far; l=left; r=right; t=top)

1: Getty Images / iStock: jondpatton

Dinosaur: 123RF.com: Mark Turner br; **Alamy Stock Photo:** Allstar Picture Library Ltd. / DreamWorks tr, Tom Bean cb, Steppenwolf clb; **Dorling Kindersley:** The American Museum of Natural History crb, Jon Hughes cra, cra/ (Euparkeria), James Kuether cla, (back poster), Senckenberg Gesellschaft Fuer Naturforschung Museum cb/ (Stegosaurus), Staatliches Museum fur Naturkunde Stuttgart crb/ (Allosaurus); **Getty Images:** The Washington Post / Bill O'Leary fbr; **Science Photo Library:** Natural History Museum, London cr, Millard H. Sharp / Science Source bl.

Cat: Alamy Stock Photo: Martin Chapman (cr/Cheetah mage). **Dreamstime.com:** Anankkml (c); Ondřej Prosick (back poster); Victor Lapaev (t); Holly Kuchera (cr). **naturepl.com:** Daniel Heuclin (cra). **Science Photo Library:** UCL, Grant Museum of Zoology (cla).

Horse: The Trustees of the British Museum: tl. Alamy Stock Photo: Paul Rollins cra; **Dreamstime.com:** Viktoria Makarova (back poster).

Fish: Alamy Stock Photo: Cbimages (clb). **Dorling Kindersley:** Colin Keates / Natural History Museum, London (tl/ Fossil); Colin Keates / Natural History Museum, London (ca); Colin Keates / Natural History Museum, London (ca/Carp Scale); Colin Keates / Natural History Museum (ca/Tarpon Fish Scale). **naturepl.com:** Andy Murch (c); Alex Mustard (cla/Striped mackerel); Nature Production (cb/White spotted pufferfish); Nature Production (cb/ White spotted puffer fish pair); Tim Fitzharris (back poster). **Galápagos Whale Shark Project:** © Jenny Waack (br). **Science Photo Library:** Ted Kinsman (ca/ Shark Skin); Peter Scoones (tl).

Shark: Alamy Stock Photo: Helmut Corneli (back poster), Reinhard Dirscherl (whale shark). **Getty Images:** Image Source / Ken Kiefer 2 (cra); Dorling Kindersley: Natural History Museum, London cb (gill rakers), cb (jaw), cb (teeth); **Getty Images:** Photographer's Choice / Georgette Douwma cb (turtle), Jeffrey L. Rotman / Photonica cla (danger sign).

Ocean: Alamy Stock Photo: Panther Media GmbH / Uebama crb, **Louisiana Governors Office (br); Corbis:** Gary Bell / zefa cl (shoal); **Getty Images / iStock:** Michael Zeigler (back poster).

Amazon Wallchart: Alamy Stock Photo: Amazon-Images fcrb, James Davis Photography bc, Pulsar Imagens (bl); **Corbis** Layne Kennedy cla; **Dreamstime.com:** 44kmos fcl, Dolphfyn crb/ (Oil Palm Fruit), Hotshotsworldwide c, cl, Isselee cr, Viktarm crb/ (Passion fruit); **Getty Images:** Gordon Wiltsie fcra, Kam & Co. fcrb/ (Bananas); **naturepl.com:** Pete Oxford (back poster), Doug Perrine clb; **Science Photo Library:** Max Alexander (bc/Protest); Sheila Terry tr; **Shutterstock.com:** GTW (br); **Source: Empresa Brasileira de Correios e Telégrafos:** cra. **Jerry Young:** cr/ (Vampire Bat).

Insect: Alamy Stock Photo: Media Drum World (back poster), Michel Gunther / Biosphoto (cb). **Dreamstime.com:** Jmrocek (cra). **Shutterstock.com:** Danielkreissl (cb/Euplagia quadripunctaria); **Dorling Kindersley:** Colin Keates / Natural History Museum, London tr, c, cl, cb, crb, bc, bl; Booth Museum of Natural History, Brighton clb.

Reptile: Dreamstime.com: Wayan Sumatika ca; **Dorling Kindersley:** Natural History Museum, London ftr, fcrb; **Getty Images:** Martin Harvey / Gallo Images fcr; **Getty Images / iStock:** amwu (back poster), SteveMcsweeny br; **Shutterstock.com:** EcoPrint clb.

Bird: DK Images: Natural History Museum, London ca, crb, tr; **Alamy Stock Photo:** Eureka crb (Duck), **Dreamstime.com:** Johannes Gerhardus Swanepoel bl (Ostrich); **Getty Images:** Mint Images RF / David Schultz (back poster).

Rock & Mineral: 123RF.com: 1xpert (c); Alamy Stock Photo: Heritage Image Partnership Ltd / Werner Forman Archive / British Museum, London bc/ (Decorative stones); **Dorling Kindersley:** Natural History Museum, London ca/ (Pebbles), cla/ (Lead Solder), cla/ (Galena), fcl, clb, cr, clb/ (Gold), br, bc/ (Marble), bc/ (Opal), cb/ (Sapphire), cb/ (Emerald), cb/ (Aquamarine), fbl/ (All ten images), bl/ (Diamonds), Natural History Museum, London cra/ (Ropy Lava), Natural History Museum, London crb/ (Plants - coal's raw ingredients), Natural History Museum, London bc, Natural History Museum, London bc/ (Knife), Natural History Museum, London cb/ (Quartz), Rob Reichenfeld ca; **Dreamstime.com:** Aitor Muñoz Muñoz cr; **Getty Images / iStock:** E+ / Kanawa_Studio (back poster).

Crystal & Gem: PunchStock Photodisc c. **Science Photo Library:** MSF / Javier Trueba (back poster).

Fossil: Alamy Stock Photo: Enrico Della Pietra cl, Science History mages / Photo Researchers tl; **Dorling Kindersley:** Natural History Museum, London tr, cra, cla/ (shells and pebbles), cla, ca / (Tribrachidium), ca, c, clb/ (coral), clb/ (bryozoa), clb / (shell), clb, crb/ (human skull), crb/ (chimpanzee skull), crb/ (brushes); crb, bl, bc, bc/ (hammer), br (Lens), br, Colin Keates / Natural History Museum, London cb, Gary Ombler / Senckenberg Gesellschaft Fuer Naturforschung Museum cr; **Getty Images:** Taxi / Peter Scoones crb/ (blue fish).

Volcano & Earthquake: Alamy Stock Photo: Imaginechina Limited (bc); **DK Images:** Museo Archeologico Nazionale di Napoli cr; Natural History Museum, London clb (aa lava), cra (pyroclastic debris); **Getty Images:** 500px / KristjanKristinsson (back poster); Image Bank / G. Brad Lewis cla (Pahoehoe flow); National Geographic / Klaus Nigge ca; **Getty Images / iStock:** Bestgreenscreen (bc/Thermal Camera); **Science Photo Library:** Gary Hincks (tl).

Weather: Alamy Images: Michael Freeman br, Zoonar GmbH (ca); David R. Frazier Photolibrary Inc (cb); David J. Green (cra); **BAE Systems Regional Aircraft:** fcl (Aircraft); **Corbis** crb; Lynsey Addario bl; Roger Ressmeyer cr (Lightning); **Dreamstime.com:** Andrei Radzkou (ca/Cirrostratus clouds); Tomislav Ladisic (cla/ Sunset); Parkpoom4 (cla/Sunrise). **Getty Images / iStock:** Mdesigner125 (back poster); **FAAM / Doug Anderson, Maureen Smith & Met Office, UK:** cl; **Science Photo Library:** NOAA cl (Storm).

Hurricane & Tornado: Alamy Images: Kelton Halbert c, Don Mennig br (Climate change); Reven T.C. Wurman cra; **The Trustees of the British Museum:** cla/ (Maori Kite); **Corbis:** Warren Faidley cla; **Dreamstime.com:** Nickolayv tl; **Getty Images:** 500px Prime / Chad Cowan (back poster), AFP / Bertrand Guay tr (Weather balloon), AFP / Tony Karumba cr; Photographer's Choice RF / Nacivet cl; **Science Photo Library:** Roger Hill bc (Tornado phases).

Natural Disaster: Alamy Stock Photo: Universal Images Group North America LLC / DeAgostini / DEA PICTURE LIBRARY (back poster); **Corbis** Arno Balzarini / epa (fclb), Alberto Garcia (bl), Rafiqur Rahman / Reuters (c), Alamy Stock Photo: Ed Darack / RGB Ventures / SuperStock (crb) Wave (cr); **Dorling Kindersley:** Aberdeen Fire Department, Maryland (fcr); **Getty Images:** Jeff Hunter / The mage Bank (tr) / (Background), Tom Pfeiffer / VolcanoDiscovery / Photographer's Choice (b), JIJI Press / AFP (cl); **NASA** Scientific Visualization Studio Collection (cr) / (hurricane); **NASA Goddard Space Flight Center:** (crb); **U.S. Geological Survey:** Walter Mooney (cla); **Courtesy of U.S. Army:** Capt. Daniel A. Hill, 49th PAD (clb), Tech. Sgt. James B. Pritchett (tr).

Wonders of the world: Alamy Stock Photo: F1online digitale Bildagentur GmbH (bc/Petra Wadi); Jack Sullivan (ca/ Dead Sea); Gavin Hellier / Robertharding (crb/Angkor Wat). **Dorling Kindersley:** Alan Keohane / Hopi Learning Centre, Arizona (cra/ Kachina Doll). **Dreamstime.com:** Rodrigolab (back poster); Thomas Humeau (clb/Fuji); Witr (cb/Pyramids); Sofiaworld (cb/Wall of China); Danilo Mongiello (bl/Machu pichu); Engin Korkmaz (br/Burj Khalifa); Pniesen (tr/Coral). **Getty Images / iStock:** Kojihirano (ca/ Grand Canyon); Nicolamargaret (c); Mlenny (clb/Easter Island). **Getty Images:** Anton Petrus (ca/Salar de Uyuni); Guy Vanderelst (crb/Colosseum). **Science Photo Library:** JAVIER TRUEBA / MSF (tr/Cave of Crystals). **Shutterstock.com:** Peter Giovannini / imageBROKER (tl). **SuperStock:** Age fotostock (cra/Namib Desert).

Periodic Table: Alamy Stock Photo: Aflo Co. Ltd. 113, dpa picture alliance archive 110, Everett Collection Historical 96, Ewing Galloway 84, 88, The Granger Collection bl, Heritage Image Partnership Ltd 101, ITAR-TASS Photo Agency 118, Keystone Pictures USA 99, Science History Images 105, 97, 106, Sputnik 114; **Bridgeman Images:** icolaus Copernicus Museum, Frombork, Poland 112; **Dorling Kindersley:** Ruth Jenkinson / RGB Research Limited 1, 8, 3, 4, 11, 12, 2, 7, 10, 18, 5, 9, 13, 14, 15, 16, 17, 19, 20, 21, 22, 23, 24, 25, 26, 27, 28, 29, 30, 31, 32, 33, 34, 35, 36, 54, 37, 38, 39, 40, 41, 42, 43, 44, 45, 46, 47, 48, 49, 50, 51, 52, 53, 55, 56, 72, 73, 74, 75, 76, 77, 78, 79, 80, 81, 82, 83, 86, 57, 58, 59, 60, 62, 63, 64, 65, 66, 67, 68, 69, 70, 71, 90, 92; **Dreamstime.com:** Epitavi (back poster). **Alamy Stock Photo:** GL Archive 102; **Fotolia:** apttone 6; **Getty Images:** Bettmann 107, Bettmann, Gamma-Keystone 87, Keystone 85, Scientifica 94, Universal Images Group 104; **Lawrence Berkeley National Laboratory:** 103; **Science Photo Library:** American Institute of Physics 100, Emilio Segre Visual Archive / American Institute of Physics 109, David Parker 108; **US Department of Energy:** 98.

Planets: ESA: NASA / JHU Applied Physics Lab / Carnegie Inst. Washington tr; **NASA and The Hubble Heritage Team (AURA/ STScI): cr; NASA:** b, Enhanced image by Gerald Eichstädt based on images provided courtesy of NASA / JPL-Caltech / SwRI / MSSS (back poster), JPL-Caltech / MSSS ca, Johns Hopkins University Applied Physics Laboratory / Southwest Research Institute cb, Johns Hopkins University Applied Physics Laboratory / Southwest Research Institute cb/ (Pluto), JPL-Caltech crb, JPL-Caltech cra, SDO tl.

Human Body: DK Images: Denoyer - Geppert Intl. br (inner ear). **Dreamstime.com** Albund (crb/ Background); Yevgeniy Repiashenko (crb/Girl); Mamahoohooba (bl). **Science Photo Library:** ftr (cell division).

Train: Alamy: cl, DPA Picture Alliance (bc); imageBROKER.com GmbH & Co. KG / Klaus Rainer Krieger (c). **Corbis** José Fuste Raga / zefa br. **DK Images:** National Railway Museum, York cla (Stephenson's Rocket), clb (diesel locomotive), clb (train tickets), cl (tea set), cl (ticket clippers), cra (wheel), tr (workman's pick); Science Museum, London tl (Trevithick's train); **Dreamstime.com:** Sean Pavone (back poster).

Flight: Airbus: Master Films - Hervé Goussé cr; **Alamy Stock Photo:** Felix Images (bc/Bell X-1); **NASA Photo** (back poster), MediaWorldImages br, Thierry GRUN - Aero bl; **Corbis:** Swim Ink 2, LLC **ftr; Dorling Kindersley:** Courtesy of The Shuttleworth Collection, Bedfordshire cla (LVG CVI); Imperial War Museum, London fcl; **Getty Images:** Mark Harwood bc; Library of Congress / Science Faction tl ('Flyer'); Taxi bl (balloon).

Ancient Egypt: Alamy Stock Photo: PA Media Pte Ltd/ Pictures From History cr (The Rosetta Stone); **Dorling Kindersley:** British Museum be, fcra (Papyrus), tl; Wellcome Institute / Science Museum, London cb; Bolton Library and Museum Services / Norman Taylor cra (Nefertiti); **Dreamstime.com: Michal Janoek / Wesleyc1701** (back poster). Pius Lee crb (Pyramid). **Getty Images:** De Agostini / DEA / A. Jemolo cla (Cattle count).

Ancient Greece: Alamy Stock Photo: David Ball clb; Jan Wlodarczyk cla, Hercules Milas (back poster); **© The Trustees of the British Museum. All rights reserved.:** c; **Corbis:** David Lees br; **DK Images:** British Library fclb (Pottery); British Museum cl; Dr John Coates crb (Boat); **Dreamstime. com:** Maart cla/ (Columns); **Getty Images:** Moment / Joe Daniel Price tr.

Ancient Rome: Alamy Stock Photo: AGF Srl / Alessandro Serrano' (back poster); **Azoor Photo (br). DK Images:** British Museum cl; Ermine Street Guard c, cb, clb (pilum), clb (sword and dagger), tc; Rough Guides tl; **Dreamstime.com:** crb; **Getty Images:** Bridgeman Art Library fbr, **Science & Society Picture Library** (cra).

Viking: Alamy Images: Terry Allen crb, Makno clb (fire); **Bridgeman Images:** Bibliothèque Nationale, Paris, France ftl; Tapestry by Mabelle Linnea Holmes / Jamestown-Yorktown Educational Trust, VA, USA tr; **DK Images / Peter Anderson:** Danish National Museum cb (arm-ring), clb (pin), clb (Thor's hammer), crb (brooch), crb (key), fbr (Jelling); Courtesy of the Statens Historiska Museum, Stockholm clb (Frey), cr (picture stone), tl; Courtesy of the Universitets Oldsaksamling, Oslo br (chest), fcl (helmet), fbl; York Museums Trust (Yorkshire Museum)cra (Quern); **DK Images / Andrew McRobb:** fcr (wheat); **Werner Forman Archive:** fcra (anchor).

Knight: DK Images: Judith Miller/Otford Antiques and Collectors Centre 1bl (Brooch); Judith Miller/Sloan's 1tr; **Michael Holford:** 1clb (Pilgrimage). **Shutterstock.com:** Pic Media Aus (back poster).

Titanic: Alamy Stock Photo: Shawshots (back poster); © WALT DISNEY PICTURES / AJ Pics (br) **Dorling Kindersley:** © NMM / National Museums and Galleries on Merseyside c, Rough Guides cl (Titanic interior); **Getty Images:** Topical Press Agency / Hulton Archive bl.

World War I: Alamy Stock Photo: Military Images cla. **Corbis:** tr. **Dorling Kindersley:** Imperial War Museum, London c, cr, (back poster); Gary Ombler / Fort Nelson (crb); **Getty Images:** Bettmann br.

World War II: Alamy Stock Photo: Simon Pocklington (back poster); **Dorling Kindersley:** Imperial War Museum, London / Andy Crawford / By kind permission of The Trustees of the Imperial War Museum, London cr, (br) (atomic bomb); Royal Artillery Historical Trust cla (Lee Enfield), cla (Tommy Gun) **Corbis** fclb (Pearl Harbor); **Getty Images:** API/Gamma-Rapho tr.

A *Stegosaurus* is cornered by three *Allosaurus*.

DINOSAUR

Dinosaurs began to evolve more than 240 million years ago. This extraordinary group of reptiles ranged from gigantic to tiny in size. Some dinosaurs were fierce hunters; others were peaceful plant-eaters. Birds are living dinosaurs and the only dinosaur group to have survived a mass extinction 66 million years ago.

Classification of dinosaurs

Scientists usually divide dinosaurs into two groups according to their hip bones. In most saurischian dinosaurs, a hip bone called the pubis pointed forwards. In ornithischian dinosaurs, the pubis sloped down and back like that of a bird.

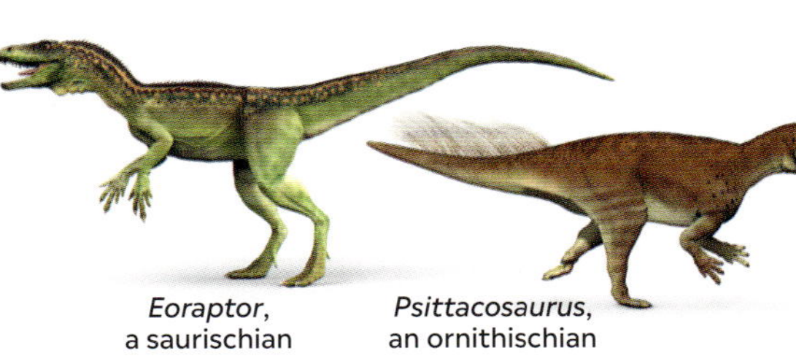

Eoraptor, a saurischian

Psittacosaurus, an ornithischian

End of an era

Around 66 million years ago, all dinosaurs, except for the small theropods that we know as birds, died out. This mass extinction was caused by a catastrophic asteroid impact.

The Age of Dinosaurs

Geologists divide Earth's history into time zones, from its origin around 4,600 million years ago (mya) to the present day. The Age of Dinosaurs was during the Mesozoic Era, which is divided into three periods: Triassic, Jurassic, and Cretaceous.

THE AGE OF DINOSAURS

Modern humans appeared 300,000 years ago.

Dinosaur features

Dinosaurs had many shared traits that help classify them, such as an open hip socket for their upright stance. Some had scaly skin while others had feathers. *Monolophosaurus* had many of the characteristics of the first dinosaurs, such as bipedal (two-legged) gait.

Neck with S-shaped curve

Scaly skin

Long, serrated teeth lined the jaws.

Upright hindlimb

Long tail counterbalanced the neck and head.

Recurved claws

Hand with three digits

Weight-bearing toes

Monolophosaurus, a theropod (meat-eater)

Proterosuchus

A sprawling walker

Proterosuchus was a close cousin of the archosaurs (ruling reptiles). Unlike the dinosaurs, it had limbs that stuck out sideways and walked in a sprawling way, like crocodiles.

Archosaur cousin

The agile *Euparkeria* was a descendant of the early sprawling archosaurs. It walked on all fours but, like the dinosaurs, it probably reared up on its hindlegs to run.

Euparkeria

Dinosaur evolution

Evolution is the process by which a species gradually adapts to its changing environment. Dinosaurs evolved from a group of reptiles called archosaurs. Early dinosaurs were two-legged hunters with grasping hands.

Dinosaur landscape

During the Age of Dinosaurs, the world changed substantially. The continents were one great landmass at first, then drifted slowly apart. The climate and vegetation also changed over time.

Triassic Period

Earth's land formed one giant supercontinent called Pangaea. Plants included ferns, horsetails, and cycads.

Jurassic Period

Pangaea broke up into two landmasses – Laurasia and Gondwana. The climate warmed, and plants included tree ginkgoes and mosses.

Cretaceous Period

Gondwana and Laurasia split into smaller landmasses that eventually became the continents we know today. Flowering plants appeared.

Fossils

We know about dinosaurs mainly from their fossilized bones. Sometimes the imprints of a dinosaur's soft body parts, such as its skin and muscles, also survive.

Fossilized dinosaur footprints, also known as ichnites

Dinosaur footprints

Fossilized dinosaur footprints help scientists to work out the sizes of dinosaurs and how they moved.

Dinosaur mummy

This *Edmontosaurus* fossil has traces of the animal's skin over its fossilized bones. An impression of the skin was preserved by river mud that later turned to rock.

Skin impression

Mummified *Edmontosaurus*

Dinosaur weapons

Plant-eating dinosaurs evolved all kinds of weapons that helped them fight competitors or predators. *Triceratops* had a large, bony frill at the back of its skull and sharp horns. Some ankylosaurs had large bony tail clubs. Many plant-eaters had armour-plated skin.

Back plate

Neck plate

Rib

Spiked tail

Tail bone

Stegosaurus skeleton

Plated dinosaur

Stegosaurus was the largest stegosaur (plated dinosaur). Most stegosaurs sported two rows of tall spikes, but *Stegosaurus* had an alternating double row of plates along its neck, back, and tail.

Shield-shaped skull

Long, sharp brow horn

Small nose horn

Narrow, horny beak

Triceratops skeleton

Hollow made skull less heavy.

Eye socket

Allosaurus skull

Powerful lower jaw

Allosaurus skull

Sturdy bones in *Allosaurus's* huge skull supported its jaw muscles and bladelike teeth. The jaw joint acted like scissors to tear off flesh.

Meat-eaters

Some theropods (meat-eating dinosaurs) had powerful jaws for killing and tearing up large prey. Jaws of the huge *Allosaurus* and *Tyrannosaurus* were lined with knifelike teeth that could slice through flesh. Others had jaws adapted for catching fish or insects.

Dinosaur young

Dinosaurs hatched from eggs. By studying a fossil eggshell, scientists can tell which type of dinosaur laid the egg.

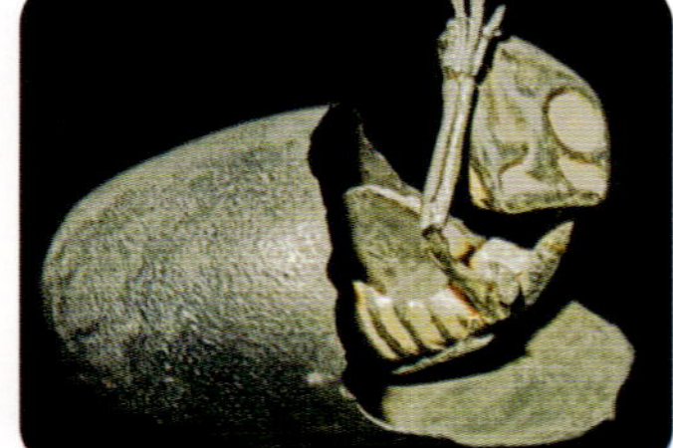

Feathered wings

Archaeopteryx

Clawed toe

Feathered dinosaurs

Archaeopteryx, a prehistoric cousin of modern birds, had feathered wings. The first feather-like structures might have kept the body warm.

Feathered tail

Feathered arm

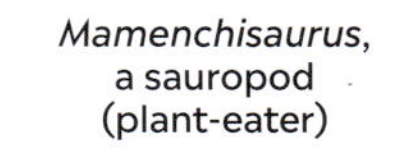

Velociraptor

Scientists found small bumps on a fossil of the *Velociraptor*. In birds, these bumps anchor feathers to the bone, so it's probable that *Velociraptor* was feathered as well.

Plant-eaters

Plant-eating dinosaurs had jaws, teeth, and guts suited to cropping, chewing, and digesting vegetation. Some, like the huge *Brachiosaurus* and *Mamenchisaurus*, had long necks to reach into tall trees.

Mamenchisaurus, a sauropod (plant-eater)

Lawnmower

Nigersaurus's wide, shovel-shaped mouth was adapted for grazing on low-growing plants.

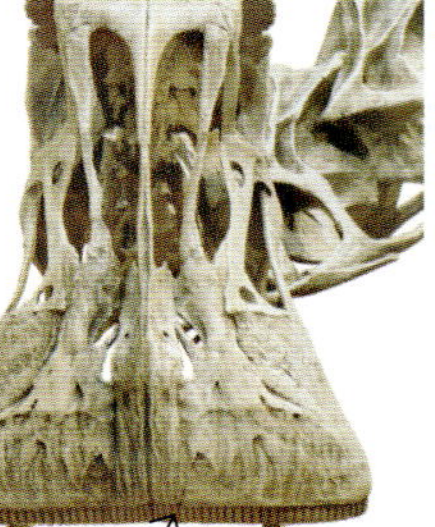

Nigersaurus skull

Rows of teeth, regularly replaced

A Siberian tiger

CAT

All cats belong to one family, the Felidae. They have the typical features of mammals – fur, warm blood, a protective skeleton, and an upright walk. Cats are carnivores (meat-eaters) and mostly live and hunt on their own.

Cats' long tails aid balance.

Early cats
The first true cats (felids) evolved 35 million years ago. Some species of cat, such as the North American *Smilodon*, evolved enormous, sabre-shaped teeth for stabbing prey.

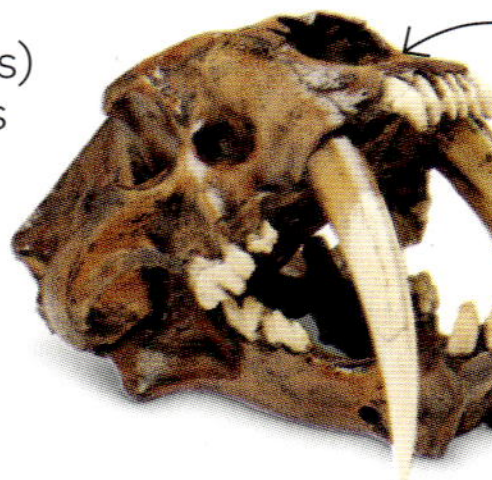

Most of Smilodon's skull was made up of its jaws and teeth.

Tree climbers
Leopards are the biggest cats to climb trees frequently, and often rest comfortably on the branches. They also drag their prey high up above the ground, away from other predators.

Cat and its habitat
The jaguar is the only large cat found on the American continent. A skilled hunter, it kills tapirs, turtles, and other small animals. It can even hunt under water.

Clouded leopard

Cheetah

The cat family
The cat family includes the domesticated cat and 40 species of wildcat, divided into four groups – the small cats, the large cats, the cheetah, and the clouded leopard.

Plains cat
The caracal lives on the African plains. With its long legs, it is fairly speedy over short distances.

Forest feline
Margays are solitary hunters, and have huge eyes for night-hunting.

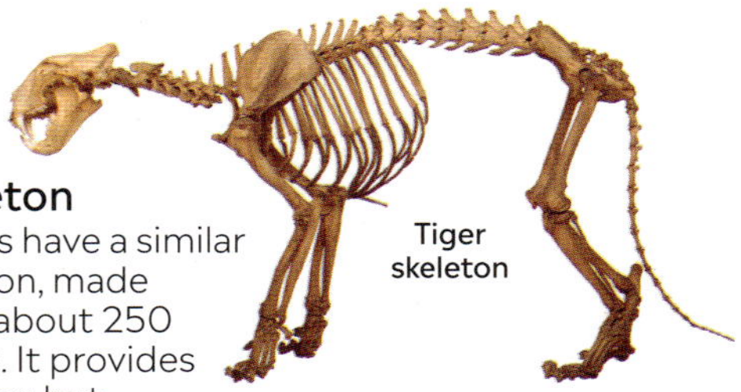

Skeleton
All cats have a similar skeleton, made up of about 250 bones. It provides a strong but flexible framework that protects the soft parts of a cat's body but also allows it to move with great agility.

Tiger skeleton

Hello kitty
Cats mark their territory by spraying their urine and depositing droppings. They exchange scents by rubbing and licking each other.

Mountain cats
The lynx, bobcat, and puma (also called the cougar) are some of the small cats. Bobcats and pumas are found in the Americas. The lynx lives in North America, Europe, and Asia.

Puma

The biggest cat
Tigers are the most powerful of all cats. They stalk their prey, hunt alone, and defend their territories from intruders. Today, tigers are an endangered species.

Striped coat provides camouflage in forests and grasslands.

Agility
All cats can leap with great power. They stalk their prey, then pounce onto the animal's back, and finally bite its neck to kill.

The runner
The cheetah is the fastest land animal in the world and can run at a speed of 96 kph (60 mph). It kills its prey by stalking and chasing it down.

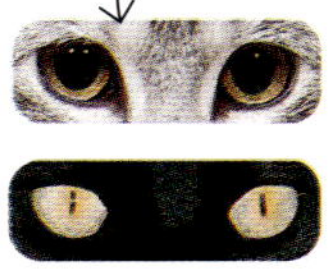

Myths and legends
The ancient Egyptians worshipped the cat goddess Bastet (right), who was associated with happiness and warmth. In medieval Europe, cats were linked with witchcraft and the Devil.

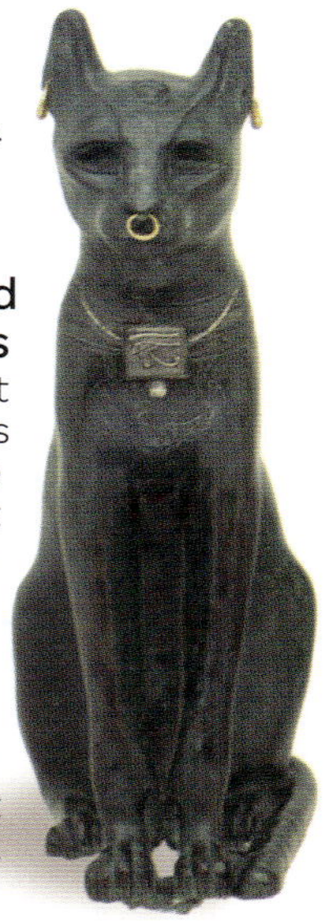

Expanded pupils

Seeing in the dark
Cats have excellent night vision. Their pupils expand in the dark to let in as much light as possible.

The exterior
Wildcats have a soft undercoat for insulation and a topcoat of hairs carrying the coat's spotted or striped pattern.

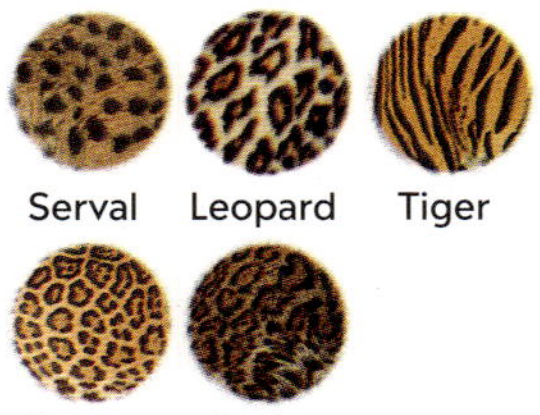

Serval | Leopard | Tiger | Jaguar | Ocelot

Caring for their young
The young of the large cats are called cubs, while those of the small cats are called kittens. The mother produces milk to feed her young and looks after them on her own.

Caring for your cat
If possible, domesticated cats should be allowed outside to explore their territory. They should also be vaccinated against diseases.

A mane makes the lion look even bigger than it really is.

Grooming
Cats spend a lot of time licking their fur with their rough tongues, pulling bits of dirt from their feet, and wiping their face and ears with their paws.

Lion
Today, lions are found only in Africa and in the Gir forest in India. A family group of lions is called a pride.

A male rules the pride, but the females do most of the hunting.

Serval

Solitary hunters
Most cats are solitary hunters (except lions and cheetahs) and can detect prey by sound and scent before they even see it.

A lioness has no mane as it would slow down her ability to hunt.

A lioness is smaller and more agile than a lion.

A Vladimir Heavy Draft horse

HORSE

All members of the horse family, including zebras and asses, are equids. In the wild, equids live in herds, feed on grass or shrubs, and run to escape predators. All 400 breeds of domestic horse belong to the species *Equus caballus*.

Gear carried in a pack on mule's back

Beasts of burden
Wild horses were first domesticated in present-day Russia about 6,000 years ago. This stone frieze, from 2,600 years ago, shows the Assyrians using mules to carry hunting gear.

Kulan – a type of Asian wild ass
Poitou donkey
Common (plains) zebra

The horse family
The horse family also includes two species of Asian wild ass (the onager and the kiang), the African wild ass (the ancestor of the domestic donkey), and the zebras.

Parts of a horse
Horses have long legs to gallop fast. Their elongated skulls contain grinding teeth, for grazing, and the sensitive smell organs. Their eyes are set far up in the skull and positioned on the sides of the head for all-round vision. The various parts of a horse are called the "points". The overall shape and appearance of a horse is called its conformation.

Alert ears to listen for danger
Forelock
Muzzle
Mane
Height at withers 17.3 hands high – 180 cm (71 in)
Rump
Belly
Thigh
Elbow
Hock
Flank
Forearm
Chest
Feathered hoof
Fetlock
Knee
Coronet
Pastern
Hoof
Cannon bone

Ten-year-old Shire mother and her five-week-old foal

Mare and foal
A mare carries young in her womb for 11 months. Within an hour of birth, the foal will stand and soon run. This helps it keep up with the herd. A mare suckles her foal for around 10 months, but it grazes after a few weeks.

Hands high
A horse's height is measured in "hands". One hand (the width of an adult's hand) is equal to 10.16 cm (4 in).

Running wild
These horses from the Camargue in the south of France are described as "feral". Feral herds were once domesticated stock but now live and breed in the wild.

Senses and behaviour
Equids have highly developed senses of sight, hearing, and scent, and retain the instincts and behaviour of their wild ancestors.

Ears pointing back shows submission, or fear.

Ears pointing forwards show interest.

One ear forwards, one back shows uncertainty.

Ear positions
Horses can move their ears separately, to pick up sounds and transmit visual signals. The position of the ears also indicates their mood.

Hooves and horseshoes
The hooves of a domestic horse are made of keratin. They are fitted with metal horseshoes by a farrier, to stop them from splitting, breaking, or becoming diseased.

Old shoe and nails

Markings
The white markings on a horse's face have different names, such as star, stripe, and blaze, based on their shape and size.

Star
Danish Warmblood

Blaze
Gelderlander

Stripe
Oldenburg

Shoeing a horse
The farrier levers off the worn horseshoe, then clips and files the hoof. The new shoe is pressed onto the foot and nailed in place.

Farrier's tools

Iron shoe is heated and then cooled to check the fit.

Work horses
In Europe and Asia, the "age of the horse" lasted from ancient Greek and Roman times until the 19th century. During this period, horses were used for transport, hauling wood, and agricultural work.

Cog
Giant iron fly-wheel attached to iron rod, or shaft
Heavy collar
Grinding stones hidden underground
Shaft attached to grinding stones

Horse power
This Shire horse is walking in a circle, pulling a rope to turn a mill wheel that grinds grain into flour. Horse-mills (mills using horses as a power source) were also used to pump water from wells.

Lasso for roping cattle

Palomino

The round-up
The wild horses of North America went extinct 10,000 years ago. The first domesticated horses in the Americas came with Christopher Columbus in 1492. Since then, they have been used in transport, hunting, and for driving cattle.

Clydesdale drum horse from the British Army's Household Cavalry

Pure silver drums

War horses
People have used horses in wars for the last 5,000 years. Drum-carrying horses are still used in processions today.

Colours and breeds
Horses are bred in different colours. The legs, mane, and tail can be a different colour from the body. Horses are grouped into three types: ponies, light horses, and heavy horses.

Black – Ariegeois
Dun – Fjord
Palomino – Haflinger

Ponies
A pony has a smaller build than a light horse, and measures up to 14.2 hands high, or 148 cm (58 in).

Bay – Cleveland Bay
Skewbald (large white patches on base colour) – Pinto, or Paint Horse
Dapple grey – Orlov Trotter

Light horses
Light horses were bred for riding or driving (pulling carriages). The Pinto is a riding horse, while the Cleveland Bay is a driving horse.

Chestnut – Suffolk Punch
Grey – Boulonnais

Roan – Ardennais

Heavy horses
These horses were bred for farm work and pulling heavy loads. Today, most are used in displays and shows. Breeds include the Shire and Clydesdale.

Orange-lined triggerfish swim past a school of snapper, near Miniloc Island in the Pacific Ocean.

FISH

Fish are cold-blooded aquatic creatures. They breathe with gills, are covered in scales, and swim using fins and streamlined bodies. Fish are an integral part of the ecosystems in our lakes, rivers, seas, and oceans.

Early fish

Fish first appeared in the seas around 500 million years ago. This coelacanth was thought to have died out 80 million years ago but was rediscovered in 1938.

How fish breathe

A fish draws water with dissolved oxygen into its mouth. The oxygen passes through its gills into the blood to be distributed around the body.

Gill membranes allow the water to flow through them.

What is a fish?

Fish are vertebrates that use gills to breathe and fins to steer while swimming. Some animals, such as dolphins or starfish, are often mistaken for fish.

Clown triggerfish

Fish scales

There are four main types of fish scales. Ganoids are hard and diamond-shaped. Placoids look like tiny teeth embedded in the skin. Cycloids have a smooth surface, while ctenoids have tiny teeth along the edge.

Ctenoid scales

Cycloid scales

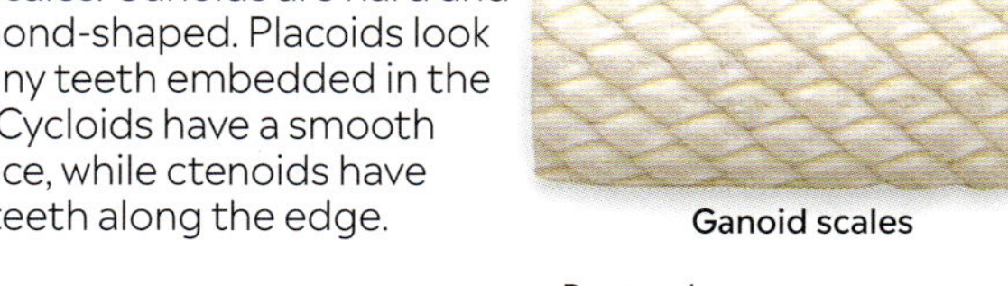
Ganoid scales

Placoid scales

Types of fish

Up to 34,000 fish species have been identified so far. They are broadly divided into three groups - bony, cartilaginous, and jawless fish.

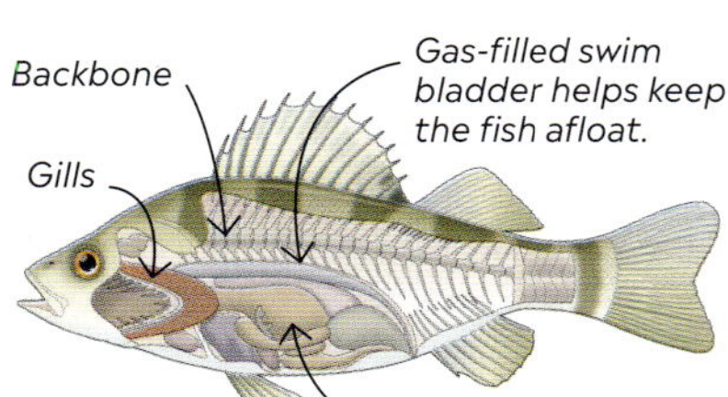

Perch

Bony fish

These have a hard, bony skeleton. Their internal organs are in the lower half of their body.

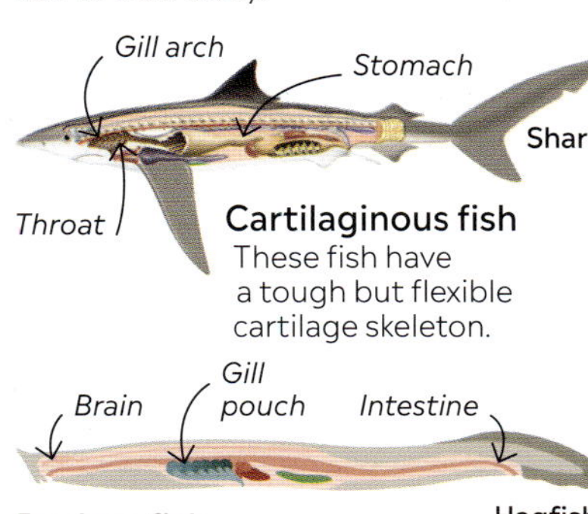

Cartilaginous fish

These fish have a tough but flexible cartilage skeleton.

Jawless fish

These have a sucker-like mouth armed with rows of rasping teeth.

How fish swim

Most fish swim in a series of S-shaped waves that start at their head and move across their body. As the wave reaches a fish's tail, the tail fin moves from side to side, pushing the fish forwards.

Striped mackerel

Pectoral fin

The wave begins as the dogfish swings its head slightly to the right.

The "peak" of the wave has passed along the body to between the pectoral and pelvic fins.

The wave's peak reaches the tail. Meanwhile, the snout has begun another wave.

Dogfish

Tomato grouper gets cleaned up.

Bluestreak cleaner wrasse

Helping each other

Close partnerships are seen among different fish species. The cleaner wrasse thoroughly cleans the grouper, and in return gets to feed on dead skin, scales, and parasites.

White-spotted pufferfish mating

The male bites the female while she lays eggs in the sandy "nest".

Finding a mate

Many fish species carry out dramatic courtship routines to attract a mate. The male white-spotted pufferfish takes up to a week to make a sand circle. The female then lays her eggs in the centre.

Thresher shark

Long, muscular tail

Large pectoral fins

Giving birth

Bony fish tend to lay millions of eggs that are left to fend for themselves. But the cannibal bullhead fish lays only up to 200 eggs, which are then guarded by the male bullhead. Some sharks give birth to fully formed young.

Cannibal bullhead

Fish defences

The oceans are filled with predators. This porcupine fish raises its prickly spines and balloons up to twice its size to avoid being eaten.

Sharks and family

Cartilaginous fish such as sharks (above), skates, sawfish, and rays (right) are varied. Sharks are powerful meat-eaters with bodies designed to hunt fish and other sea creatures. In contrast, rays have winglike fins and flat bodies adapted for living on seabeds, where they eat shellfish and other creatures.

Thornback ray

Dappled brown colours help it hide in the sandy seabed.

Studying fish

Scientists study fish to observe their behaviour and track their numbers to make sure that they are not in danger of becoming extinct due to hunting or overfishing by humans. This majestic whale shark (the biggest fish of all) is being tagged by a diver.

A scalloped hammerhead shark

SHARK
Sharks are some of the most successful marine predators. They are one of three groups of cartilaginous fish. Most cartilaginous fish live in the sea, but a few sharks live in fresh water.
Long, pointed snout
Gill slits (openings)
Dorsal fin
Spinner shark
Mouth
Pectoral fin
Pelvic fin
Caudal (tail) fin
What is a shark?
Sharks have skeletons made of cartilage, gills for breathing, specialized teeth that can be replaced when damaged, and skin covered with toothlike placoid scales called denticles.
Toxic spine, or "sting"
Stingray
Shark relatives
Like sharks, skates and rays are cartilaginous fish. They have winglike pectoral fins joined to the head, and gill slits on the underside of the flattened body.
Pectoral fin
Nurse shark
Barbel
Shark senses
The pair of feelers, or barbels, on the nurse shark's nose means it can sense prey hiding in the sand. Barbels may also play a role in taste.
Conical snout
Great white shark
Great whites grow to more than 6 m (20 ft) long and weigh more than 2 tonnes (2.25 US tons). They are the largest predatory sharks, capable of chasing after sea lions and eating them whole. Their numbers are declining in some oceans.
Grey-black upper body
Long gill slits
Triangular-shaped dorsal fin
Rows of sharp, sawlike teeth
Hammerhead
A hammerhead's eyes are on the end of its head projections, giving it a good view as it swings its head from side to side. Sensory pores on the underside of the head also help the shark to detect prey.
Giving birth
More than 60 per cent of sharks give birth to live young. The rest, such as dogfish, lay eggs. Compared to bony fish, sharks produce fewer young at a time – from two (the sand tiger shark) to 300 (a whale shark).
Model of a great white shark
Developing dogfish
Hatching dogfish
Sickle-shaped pectoral fin
Pale underbelly
Anal fin
Crescent-shaped caudal (tail) fin
Leathery egg case
Tendril
1 Dogfish eggs
The egg case containing the baby dogfish is attached to seaweed so it is not swept away by currents.
2 Juvenile
The baby dogfish takes around nine months to develop. During this time, it gets nourishment from the yolk sac inside the egg case.
Types of shark
There are more than 500 species of shark. Most have torpedo-shaped bodies, but some bottom-dwelling species have a flattened body.
Predator's jaw
A tiger shark's jaw is only loosely connected to the skull, so the shark can push out its jaws to take a big bite.
Sharp point
Serrated edge
Shark teeth
Shark teeth are shaped for different uses. Pointed teeth spear prey, while serrated teeth are used for cutting.
Blunt head
Tapering body
Port Jackson shark
A type of horn shark, this species grows up to 1.7 m (5.6 ft) long.
Tagging sharks
Scientists tag and monitor sharks to study their movement and behaviour. By studying these fish, they can find out how best to protect them in the wild.
Acoustic tag
Shark food
Almost all sharks are meat-eaters. Their diet includes fish and other sea creatures.
Goatfish
Lobster
Sea turtle
Huge jaws up to 1 m (3.3 ft) wide
Whale shark is the biggest shark of all.
Nurse shark
This shark lives in shallow waters and uses its pectoral fins to crawl along the sea bed.
Angel shark
These flattened sharks lie partly buried on the sea bed, waiting for prey.
Tiger shark jaw
Whale shark
This filter feeder opens its mouth to scoop up plankton and other tiny creatures that drift in the sea, and expels the water through its gills.
Sharks in danger
The biggest threat to sharks is overfishing: many sharks are killed either accidentally (in nets set for bony fish) or deliberately as a food source.
Gill rakers
Gill rakers
The mouths of basking sharks are lined with bristly gill rakers that trap plankton.
Thresher shark
This species herds fish into tight shoals, then stuns them with powerful slaps of its tail.
Rows of replacement teeth
Leopard shark
This shark grows to 1.8 m (6 ft). Its spots provide camouflage in shallow waters.
Distinctive black markings
Shark fin soup
The cartilaginous fibres in shark fins are made into soup, which is regarded as a delicacy in some Asian countries.
Tiger shark
Tiger sharks hunt at night and can grow to 5.5 m (18 ft) long.
Tiger-like stripes common on younger sharks
Smooth hammerhead
This is one of 10 species of hammerhead sharks. They feed on fish, including other sharks.
Narrow head flaps

A raft of young sea lions near Santa Barbara Island, California, US

OCEAN

Seawater covers more than two-thirds of Earth's surface, in five great oceans. It is always on the move, driven by the wind, tides, and powerful currents. From warm shallows to freezing depths, the oceans are home to a great variety of plants and animals.

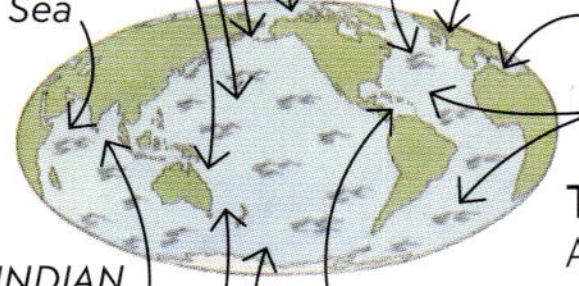

PACIFIC OCEAN
Bering Sea
ARCTIC OCEAN
Coral Sea
Sargasso Sea
Arabian Sea
Baltic Sea
Mediterranean Sea
ATLANTIC OCEAN
INDIAN OCEAN
Caribbean Sea
Tasman Sea
SOUTHERN OCEAN

The world's oceans

All the world's oceans are linked, forming a continuous mass of water. The largest expanses are the oceans; seas are smaller, and usually close to, or partly enclosed by, land.

Ocean depths

Scientists divide the oceans' waters into different zones, according to their depth. Food is scarce in the deep sea because there is no light to enable plant growth. Plants live in the sunlit waters and support a web of ocean life.

Sunlit zone

At 0–200 m (0–660 ft) below the ocean's surface, sunlight fuels the growth of plants that form the basis of the ocean food chain. Most ocean life is found here.

Twilight zone

In the twilight zone, at 200–1,000 m (660–3,300 ft), the light begins to fade – by 1,000 m (3,300 ft), it is completely dark.

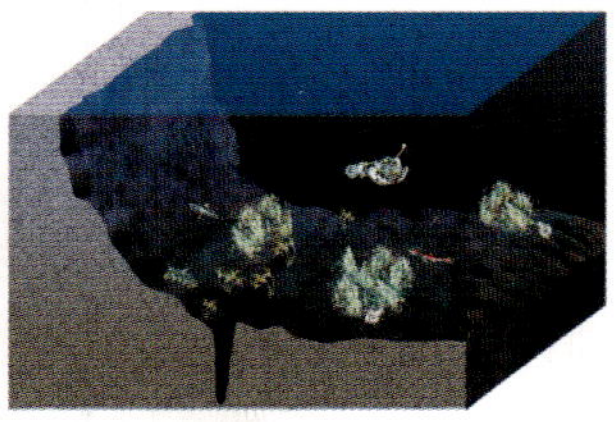

Deep-sea zone

This pitch-black and near-freezing zone lies 1,000 m (3,300 ft) below the ocean's surface and extends till the sea bed.

Vents and smokers

In some areas of the ocean floor, the vast plates that make up Earth's crust are moving apart. Cold seawater sinks into the cracks and is heated to temperatures of up to 400°C (752°F). It collects dissolved minerals, then gushes out. Some of the minerals in the water form chimneys, known as black smokers.

Plumes of hot water

Chimney

Tube worms

Giant clams

Mackerel, from the Atlantic Ocean, is harvested for its oily meat.

Fishing industry

Fish are the most popular kind of seafood, with some 90 million tonnes (99 million US tons) caught around the world each year.

Arms used for crawling along the seabed and catching food

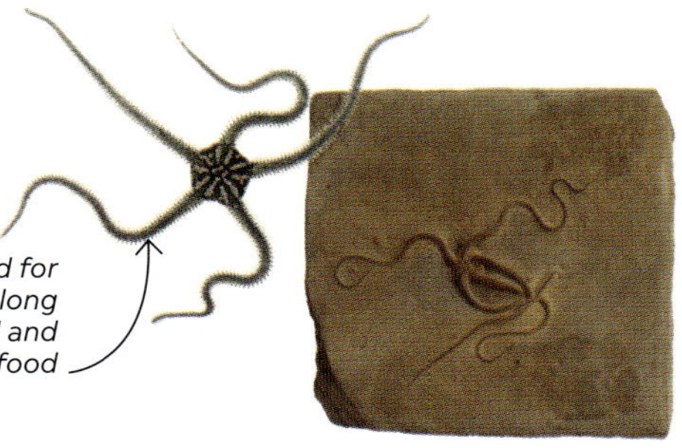

Brittle star

This 180-million-year-old fossil of a brittle star looks similar to brittle stars found today, which have five jointed arms.

Dolphin

Dolphins leap out of the water when signalling to other dolphins, hunting for food, and for fun. This marine mammal is a species of toothed whale.

Flippers used for steering

Powerful muscles move the tail up and down to move the dolphin through the water.

Life in the ocean

Animals live in all oceans, and at all depths. They include not only fish but mammals, such as whales and walruses; reptiles, such as sea turtles; and invertebrates (animals without backbones), such as jellyfish.

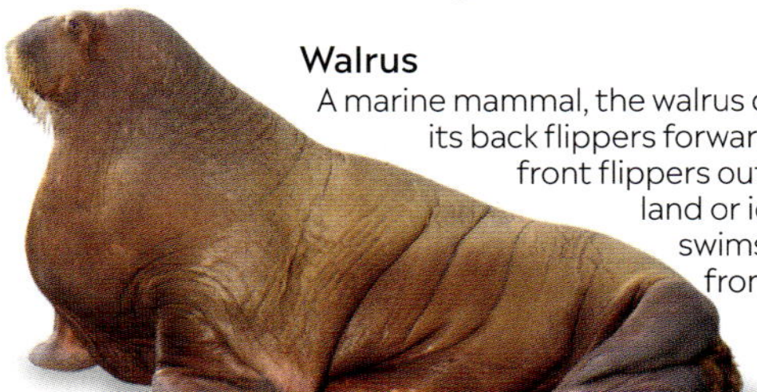

Walrus

A marine mammal, the walrus can bring its back flippers forwards and turn its front flippers outwards to walk on land or ice. In the sea, it swims using either its front or back flippers.

Shoal safety

Fish living in sunlit surface waters protect themselves from predators by forming shoals and swimming close together.

Large eye helps spot prey in the dark

Hatchet fish

Rows of light organs on the Hatchet fish's belly and tail make the fish harder to see from below in the low light of the twilight zone where it lives.

Translucent dome or bell (called a medusa)

Jellyfish

Most jellyfish, such as this box jellyfish, have tentacles with poisonous stinging cells, used to capture and immobilize prey.

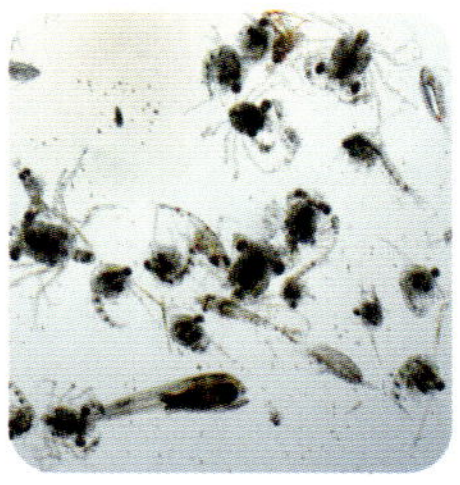

Plankton

Plankton are microscopic organisms that drift in the sea. They include phytoplankton (plants) and zooplankton (animals), which feed on the phytoplankton.

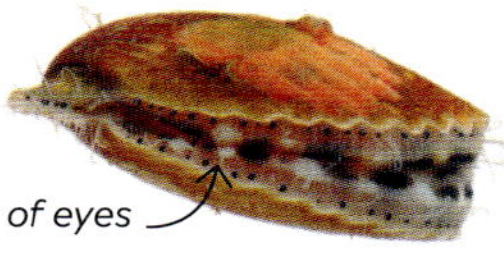

Flare stack, to burn off any gas that rises with the oil

Derrick (steel tower) holding drilling equipment

Oil platform

This oil platform has concrete legs to firmly anchor it to the sea bed. Platforms are built in sections on the shore, which are then towed out to sea.

Energy source

Valuable reservoirs of oil and gas lie beneath the sea bed. Ocean currents, waves, and tidal flow can also be harnessed to produce energy.

Wind farm

Oil reservoirs run dry, but wind turbines are a source of renewable energy. This wind farm operates in the Baltic Sea off Copenhagen, Denmark.

Row of eyes

Scallop

This clam with a hinged shell swims by squeezing jets of water from the back of its shell.

Flattened, streamlined shell

Green turtle

Sea turtles swim with their front limbs and use their back limbs as rudders to steer.

Horselike head

Seahorse

This fish usually lives among corals, sea grasses, or seaweeds, in the sunlit zone.

Tail curls around seaweed for anchorage.

Seaweed

This is a type of marine algae that uses sunlight to make food through photosynthesis.

Gas-filled bladder keeps the seaweed afloat.

Oceans in danger

Sewage and industrial waste are poisoning marine life. Overfishing has also depleted many ocean animals.

Oil spill

Huge quantities of oil are transported across the sea in tankers and pipelines. Oil spills pollute seas and shorelines, and can kill seabirds and mammals.

Coral reef

Coral reefs are delicate ecosystems teeming with various forms of life. They are under threat from global warming, pollution, and destructive fishing methods.

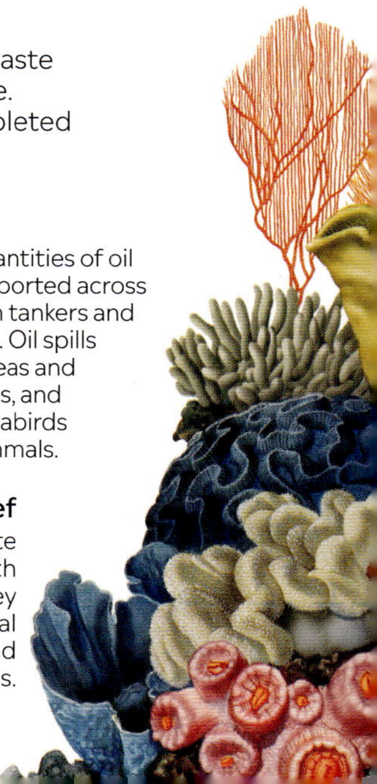

An ocelot in the Amazon Rainforest

AMAZON

South America's Amazon Rainforest is the largest in the world, and home to more than 3 million species of plant and animal. About one-fifth of the planet's fresh water is also contained in the Amazon River and its many tributaries.

Map of the Amazon Basin

Amazon Basin

The Amazon Basin is a flat region surrounded by mountains and hills on three sides. Most of it lies just south of the Equator, where the hot and wet conditions are perfect for thick forests.

Amazon River

The river

The Amazon River has the largest drainage basin in the world. More than 1,000 rivers collect the rain and water from melted mountain snow in the Amazon river system.

Macaw

Paradise tanager

In the air

Nearly 1,500 species of bird thrive in the rainforest. They range from tiny hummingbirds to large macaws that are 1 m (3.3 ft) long. Many birds are brightly coloured so they can find each other in the dense forest.

Manatee

Front limb is a flipper.

In the river

The waters of the Amazon River are home to a great variety of life, such as bull sharks, dolphins, and manatees (or sea cows).

Rosette spots help the jaguar stay hidden in thick foliage.

Jaguar

Mandioca stamp

Myth and magic

The people of the Amazon have many myths. One explains how the gods gave their ancestors the gift of food in the form of mandioca, or the cassava root.

Ancient civilizations

The Amazon region has been home to several great civilizations, such as the Inca Empire. This mummy belongs to the Chachapoya people, who lived in the cloud forests of Peru.

This mummy was buried in a cliff-top cave.

Biodiversity

No one really knows how many species live in the Amazon Rainforest. On average one new species is discovered every two days. There is a huge variety of beetles and frogs, while the river alone contains about one-sixth of Earth's fish species.

Beasts of prey

Vampire bat

The Amazon Rainforest's predators come in all shapes and sizes. The jaguar is one of the largest, but the jungle also contains deadly hunting spiders, snakes, such as the emerald tree boa, and caimans. There is even a vampire bat, which bites the flesh of animals and drinks their blood.

Colour helps snake camouflage itself among the leaves.

Emerald tree boa

Cultivation and farming

Fruits and nuts from many of the Amazon Rainforest's indigenous plants are exported around the world. However, clearing rainforest trees to grow oil palm trees for palm oil is greatly harming the region.

Bananas

Palm oil

Passion fruit

Indigenous peoples

People have been living along the Amazon for at least 12,500 years. Today, there are more than 400 tribes in the region. They have their own traditions, and a way of life that has changed little in centuries, even as they adapt to modern times.

A woman from the Yanomami tribe weaves a basket from leaves.

"Jaguar" dancers perform at a Brazilian carnival.

Life in the Amazon

About 10 million people live in the Amazon Basin, which is divided between nine countries. Most Amazonians live in cities, but also celebrate their unique rainforest culture.

Endangered lives

The rainforest is home to thousands of species that live nowhere else on Earth. Human activities, such as logging, farming, and hunting are damaging the area's natural habitats, and many of the region's species are in danger of becoming extinct.

Indigenous climate justice campaign

Save our homes

The Indigenous peoples of the Amazon region are threatened by industry and climate change and have to fight to protect their homes. Deforestation takes away shelter from the Sun, increases temperatures, and can change rain patterns.

Foot sole helps grip rough bark.

The bald uakari's red face

Uakari monkey, a vulnerable species

A devil's flower mantis

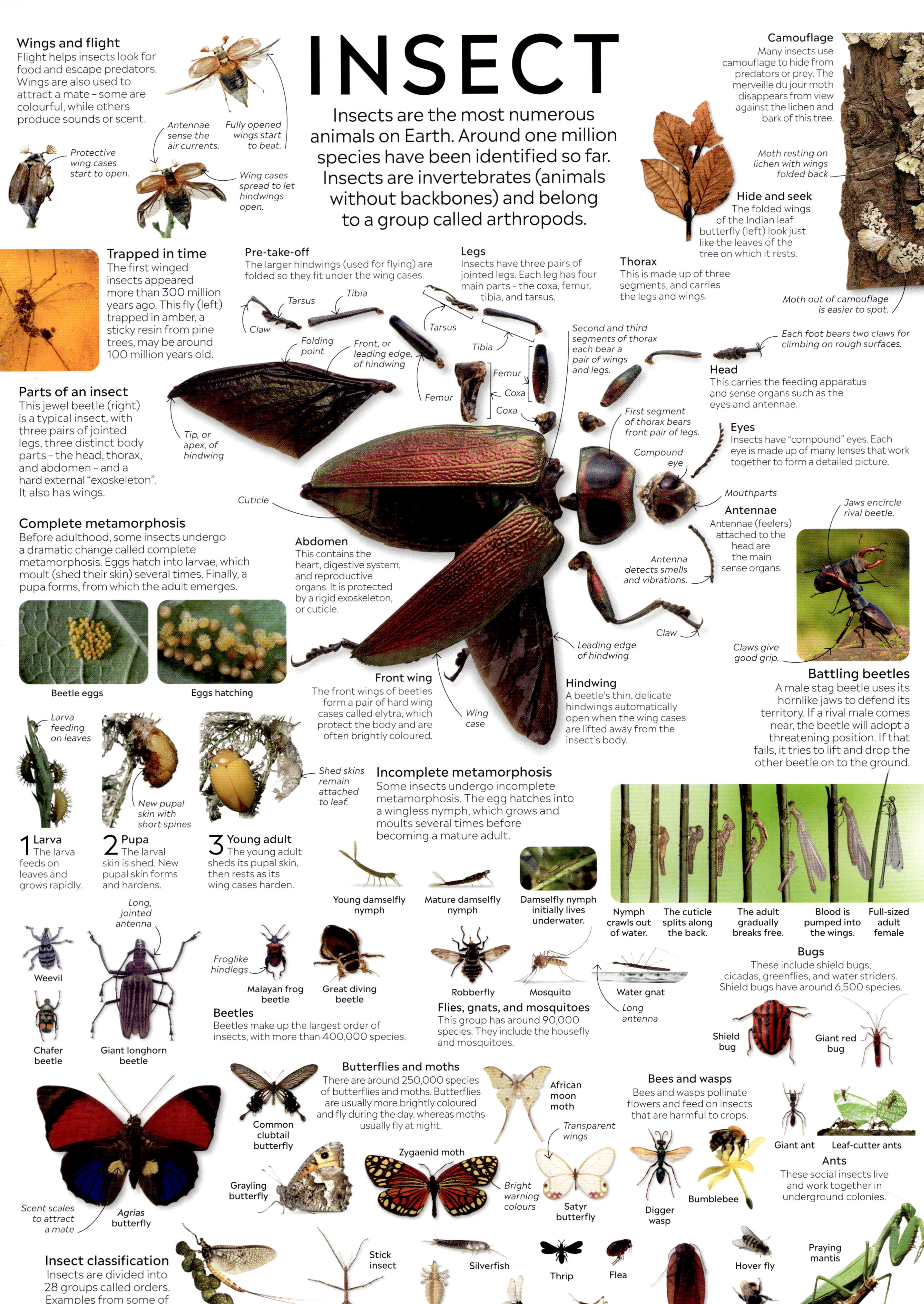
INSECT
Insects are the most numerous animals on Earth. Around one million species have been identified so far. Insects are invertebrates (animals without backbones) and belong to a group called arthropods.
Wings and flight
Flight helps insects look for food and escape predators. Wings are also used to attract a mate - some are colourful, while others produce sounds or scent.
Protective wing cases start to open.
Antennae sense the air currents.
Fully opened wings start to beat.
Wing cases spread to let hindwings open.
Camouflage
Many insects use camouflage to hide from predators or prey. The merveille du jour moth disappears from view against the lichen and bark of this tree.
Moth resting on lichen with wings folded back
Hide and seek
The folded wings of the Indian leaf butterfly (left) look just like the leaves of the tree on which it rests.
Moth out of camouflage is easier to spot.
Trapped in time
The first winged insects appeared more than 300 million years ago. This fly (left) trapped in amber, a sticky resin from pine trees, may be around 100 million years old.
Pre-take-off
The larger hindwings (used for flying) are folded so they fit under the wing cases.
Legs
Insects have three pairs of jointed legs. Each leg has four main parts - the coxa, femur, tibia, and tarsus.
Thorax
This is made up of three segments, and carries the legs and wings.
Tarsus
Tibia
Claw
Folding point
Front, or leading edge, of hindwing
Tarsus
Tibia
Femur
Femur
Coxa
Coxa
Second and third segments of thorax each bear a pair of wings and legs.
Each foot bears two claws for climbing on rough surfaces.
Head
This carries the feeding apparatus and sense organs such as the eyes and antennae.
Parts of an insect
This jewel beetle (right) is a typical insect, with three pairs of jointed legs, three distinct body parts - the head, thorax, and abdomen - and a hard external "exoskeleton". It also has wings.
Tip, or apex, of hindwing
First segment of thorax bears front pair of legs.
Compound eye
Eyes
Insects have "compound" eyes. Each eye is made up of many lenses that work together to form a detailed picture.
Cuticle
Mouthparts
Antennae
Antennae (feelers) attached to the head are the main sense organs.
Jaws encircle rival beetle.
Complete metamorphosis
Before adulthood, some insects undergo a dramatic change called complete metamorphosis. Eggs hatch into larvae, which moult (shed their skin) several times. Finally, a pupa forms, from which the adult emerges.
Abdomen
This contains the heart, digestive system, and reproductive organs. It is protected by a rigid exoskeleton, or cuticle.
Antenna detects smells and vibrations.
Claw
Claws give good grip.
Leading edge of hindwing
Beetle eggs
Eggs hatching
Front wing
The front wings of beetles form a pair of hard wing cases called elytra, which protect the body and are often brightly coloured.
Wing case
Hindwing
A beetle's thin, delicate hindwings automatically open when the wing cases are lifted away from the insect's body.
Battling beetles
A male stag beetle uses its hornlike jaws to defend its territory. If a rival male comes near, the beetle will adopt a threatening position. If that fails, it tries to lift and drop the other beetle on to the ground.
Larva feeding on leaves
New pupal skin with short spines
Shed skins remain attached to leaf.
1 Larva The larva feeds on leaves and grows rapidly.
2 Pupa The larval skin is shed. New pupal skin forms and hardens.
3 Young adult The young adult sheds its pupal skin, then rests as its wing cases harden.
Incomplete metamorphosis
Some insects undergo incomplete metamorphosis. The egg hatches into a wingless nymph, which grows and moults several times before becoming a mature adult.
Young damselfly nymph
Mature damselfly nymph
Damselfly nymph initially lives underwater.
Nymph crawls out of water.
The cuticle splits along the back.
The adult gradually breaks free.
Blood is pumped into the wings.
Full-sized adult female
Long, jointed antenna
Weevil
Chafer beetle
Giant longhorn beetle
Froglike hindlegs
Malayan frog beetle
Great diving beetle
Beetles
Beetles make up the largest order of insects, with more than 400,000 species.
Robberfly
Mosquito
Water gnat
Long antenna
Flies, gnats, and mosquitoes
This group has around 90,000 species. They include the housefly and mosquitoes.
Bugs
These include shield bugs, cicadas, greenflies, and water striders. Shield bugs have around 6,500 species.
Shield bug
Giant red bug
Butterflies and moths
There are around 250,000 species of butterflies and moths. Butterflies are usually more brightly coloured and fly during the day, whereas moths usually fly at night.
Common clubtail butterfly
African moon moth
Transparent wings
Bees and wasps
Bees and wasps pollinate flowers and feed on insects that are harmful to crops.
Giant ant
Leaf-cutter ants
Ants
These social insects live and work together in underground colonies.
Zygaenid moth
Grayling butterfly
Bright warning colours
Satyr butterfly
Digger wasp
Bumblebee
Scent scales to attract a mate
Agrias butterfly
Insect classification
Insects are divided into 28 groups called orders. Examples from some of these orders are shown here.
Mayfly
Stick insect
Silverfish
Human louse
Dragonfly
Thrip
Grasshopper
Flea
Cockroach
Hover fly
Bumblebee
Praying mantis

A Jackson's chameleon

REPTILE

Reptiles are vertebrates – they have backbones. The first reptiles evolved from amphibians about 340 million years ago. There are four groups of reptiles – snakes and lizards, crocodilians, turtles and tortoises, and tuatara.

Linked in

Reptiles are divided into family groups based on how closely related they are. Lizards and snakes are close relatives, while crocodilians are more closely related to birds.

Royal python

Worn-out old skin

Sinaloan milk snake

Outer skins

Reptiles have scaly and dry skins that protect their tissues. Snakes and some other reptiles shed their outer skin from time to time.

Armoured skin

Saltwater crocodile

Crocodilians

This ancient group is split into three families – crocodiles, gharials, and alligators. They have a more efficient blood circulation system than other reptile groups, and take care of their young for longer than most other reptiles.

The frill can measure up to 30 cm (12 in).

Australian frilled lizard

Defence mechanism

Reptiles ward off their enemies in many ways. Some, such as stinkpot turtles, release a foul smell. This lizard displays its spectacular ruffle-like collar when startled, to appear four times wider than its actual size.

Nile crocodile

Feeding habits

Most reptiles are meat-eaters. Tortoises, however, cannot hunt due to their slow pace, and largely feed on plants. Crocodiles are known to eat fish, but the larger ones hunt any animal that wanders close to the water's edge.

Deadly embrace

Some snakes, such as the boa constrictor, suffocate prey by coiling tightly around it, before swallowing it whole.

Boa constrictor

Snake swallows prey head-first.

Bony matter

In many reptiles, bone growth never stops, and the animal keeps growing throughout its life. Many of them have specialized skeletons – a chameleon's is adapted for life in trees and bushes.

Long, flexible tail for balance and holding onto a branch

Chameleon skeleton

Toes designed for grasping

Dating displays

Male anole lizards compete for females by displaying brightly coloured flaps of skin at each other; the larger males win and mate with the females.

Extended throat flap

Male anole lizard

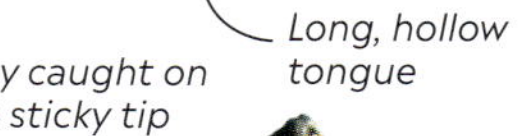

Prey caught on the sticky tip

Long, hollow tongue

Sticky tale

Chameleons have long, hollow tongues with a sticky tip. The tongue shoots out at lightning speed, and folds back once the prey has been caught.

Jackson's chameleon

Saltwater crocodile

Land and water

Reptiles are mainly land animals, but some live in water. Crocodiles hide in water, waiting to attack prey. Turtles and a few lizards also spend much of their lives submerged in water, but lay their eggs on land.

Crocodile does "tail walk" to grab prey from overhanging branches.

Hawksbill turtle shell

Shells

Land tortoises usually have high-domed or knobbly shells as a defence against predators, while turtles have flatter shells, streamlined for moving through water. Most turtles have tough scales called scutes that cover the shell's bone.

Extra senses

Reptiles have extra ways to find out about their surroundings. Some snakes have heat-sensitive pits in their lips that can detect warm-blooded prey. Others "smell" with their deeply forked tongues, helping them find a mate or detect enemies.

Indian python

Cool customers

Reptiles are cold-blooded, and rely on their surroundings for heat. Many bask in sunshine and retreat into the shade when it gets too hot.

Common agama lizard

Tokay gecko eggs

American alligator egg

African house snake egg

Eggs

Most young reptiles develop in an egg, cushioned in a bag of fluid. Some reptiles lay eggs with a leathery cover; others produce hard shells. Almost all baby reptiles look like their parents when they hatch.

An iguana has visible eardrums on both sides of its head.

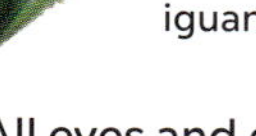

Green iguana

All eyes and ears

Lizards can see objects both up close and far away. Iguanas can actually see in colour. Most lizards hear airborne sounds through visible ear openings, with the eardrum close to the skin's surface.

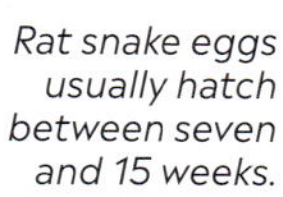

Rat snake eggs usually hatch between seven and 15 weeks.

1 The egg
Rat snake eggs are round and soft-shelled. They swell and get heavier when they absorb moisture from their surroundings.

2 Breaking out
The young reptile breaks the shell with a temporary egg tooth on its snout. It tests its surroundings by flicking its tongue.

3 Leaving the egg
The young snake begins to wriggle out of the egg. It may stay with its head poking out for a day or two.

4 Making a move
The snake leaves the egg once it is sure it is safe. Almost immediately, it can slither like an adult and fend for itself.

Emperor penguins

BIRD
There are more than 11,000 species of birds. They have feathered wings, enabling them to fly. All birds reproduce by laying eggs, and many build nests to rear their young.
Tail feathers
A bird's tail feathers help it to steer and balance. Some male birds use their long or brightly coloured tails in courtship.
Beak
Bird features
Birds have lightweight skeletons for flight. Most also have excellent vision that helps them spot prey and avoid enemies.
Scaly feet
Wing feathers
Tail feathers
Alula feathers are held open in slow flight.
Dinosaur to bird
The fossilized remains of Archaeopteryx, a prehistoric creature with feathers and clawed wings, show that birds evolved from dinosaurs.
Shaft
Parallel barbs locked together
Structure of a feather
Each feather is made up of fine, parallel strands called barbs. Feathers start growing as pulp inside tubes called sheaths, which fall away when the feather is formed.
Quill tip embedded in skin
Gull
Macaw
Outer wing feathers
These feathers provide most of the power for flight.
On the wing
A bird's wing is strong, light, and flexible. It is also slightly curved from front to back, which helps to pull the bird upwards as it flies. Bird wings vary in size and shape, but share the same basic design, as seen in this owl's wing.
Main covert feathers
Inner wing feathers
Budgerigar
Outer wing feathers
Inner wing feathers
These feathers smooth the flow of air over a bird's wings.
Pheasant
Primary flight feathers provide power as the wing moves downwards.
Secondary flight feathers form a curve to provide lift.
Inner flight feathers shape the wing into the body.
Dust baths
Birds bathe in dust or water to scour dirt from their plumage. They also use their beaks as a comb to preen their feathers.
Macaw
Peacock
Body feathers
Body feathers insulate the bird's body and also help it to identify its own kind.
Down feathers
Soft down feathers are found next to the bird's skin and help to keep the bird warm.
Cormorant skull
Mackerel
Goose skull
Buzzard skull
Strip of meat torn from prey
Fish- and meat-eaters
Birds of prey, such as buzzards, use their powerful, hooked beaks to rip apart their prey. Cormorants dive into the sea to snatch fish with their long, thin beaks.
Finch skull
Hard-cased seeds
Plant- and seed-eaters
These birds crush their food with their beaks. Plant-eaters such as geese have broad bills for tearing up grass. Finches have short, sharp bills for breaking open seeds and nuts.
Grass
Nest chamber
Cup-shaped nest
Dry grass for structure
Moss for insulation
Horse hair forms nest's cup shape
Feathers for insulation
Making a nest
Birds' nests vary hugely in size and structure. This pied wagtail's nest is made up of materials from fields and hedgerows.
Tern
Common tern
Grey heron
Curlew
Gull
Shoveler duck
Albatross
Buzzard
Tawny owl
Grouse
Jackdaw
Nightjar
Woodpecker
Blue tit
Eggs of waterbirds and waders
Seabirds often lay a single egg on a rocky ledge. Wading birds lay camouflaged eggs.
Eggs of land birds
Land birds usually lay around 12 eggs at a time.
Weaver nest
Weavers use their beaks and feet to tie knots. This enables them to weave grasses tightly into different shapes, such as a sphere or tube.
Nightingale nest
The cup-shaped nest is loosely made from reeds and leaves, and is lined with soft grass.
Hatching
A hatching bird may spend hours, or even days, breaking open its shell.
Getting ready to hatch
After 10 minutes
After 12 minutes
After 20 minutes
Duckling
Reeds
Reed warbler nest
This bird's nest, made of grass and feathers, is slung between dried stems in a reedbed. It is anchored to the reeds with "handles" like those on a basket.
Chaffinch nest
A chaffinch builds its nest using spider webs, branches, moss, lichen, and grass.
Growing up
Young blue tits grow rapidly, fuelled by a constant supply of food from their parents.
One day old
Three days old
Five days old
Nine days old
Thirteen days old
Bird groups
Arctic tern
Shorebirds and waders
These include terns, gulls, and puffins.
Ostrich
Flightless birds
These include rheas, ostriches, and cassowaries.
Mute swan
Waterfowl
Waterfowl have webbed feet and big beaks.
Roseate spoonbill
Large waders
Birds such as spoonbills and herons wade into water to find food.
Bald eagle
Birds of prey
They have hooked beaks, good eyesight, and talons.
Macaw
Parrots
These include lorikeets, parrots, and macaws.
Green wood-hoopoe
Kingfishers and hoopoes
Most of these birds eat meat.
Golden pheasant
Game birds
Game birds, such as pheasants, are hunted for their meat. They usually live on the ground.
Blue tit
Perching birds
These include swallows, crows, thrushes, warblers, and tits.
Owls
These birds of prey are usually nocturnal and have excellent night vision.
Southern boobook owl

Rainbow Mountains, Zhangye National Geopark, China

ROCK & MINERAL

Rocks are made up of the crystals of natural minerals. There are hundreds of kinds of rock, each with a unique mix of minerals that gives the rock its characteristic colour, shape, and properties. Depending on how they are formed, rocks can be igneous, sedimentary, or metamorphic.

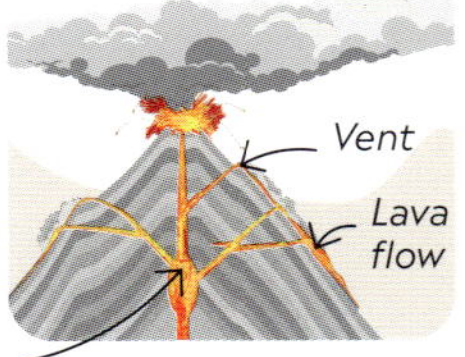

Inside a volcano
After a volcanic eruption, the lava forms different kinds of rock, depending on how fast it flows and cools.

Cutting edge of flint *Flint* *Reproduction wooden handle*

Flint tools
Flint fractures to a sharp edge, and was used by early people to make sharp tools.

Adze (10,000–4000 BCE)

Sickle (4000–2300 BCE)

Flint daggers (2750–1800 BCE)

Holes left by gas bubbles

Pumice
This igneous rock is formed from solidified lava froth. As the froth contains bubbles of gas, the rock is full of holes, and can float in water.

Ore minerals
Ore minerals are dug out of the ground in mines or quarries, and are processed to extract many useful metals.

Wind erosion
These large landforms in Monument Valley, Arizona, US, were shaped by wind-borne particles grinding away the rock.

Chemical erosion
The Parthenon in Athens, Greece, shows the effects of drastic weathering, as chemicals in the air and rain erode the stone.

Ice erosion
In mountainous regions, rock fragments frozen in a glacier's base scour the rocks beneath as the icy mass moves down a valley.

Obsidian, a natural volcanic glass

Shiny obsidian
Glassy, sharp-edged obsidian forms when lava cools so rapidly, there is no time for crystals to grow.

Basalt columns
The hexagonal pillars of the Giant's Causeway, Northern Ireland, formed when lava cooled, shrank, and cracked as it became solid basalt.

Lead solder

Galena, a lead ore

Waves and tides sort beach pebbles eroded by the sea into different sizes.

Large, coarse pebbles · Medium-sized pebbles · Fine pebbles · Finest pebbles · Quartz sand

Basaltic ropy lava

Granite

Igneous rocks
There are two types of igneous rock. Intrusive rocks, such as granite, form when magma cools slowly deep below ground. Extrusive rocks, such as basalt, form when erupted magma quickly cools at the surface.

Bornite

Chalcopyrite

Copper joint used in plumbing

Copper ore

Platinum nugget

Precious metals
Gold and silver were among the earliest metals discovered. Silver is mined with copper, lead, and zinc. Gold is often found in veins of quartz. Platinum, rarer and more valuable than gold, occurs in a variety of minerals.

Gold mixed with quartz

Chalk, a powdery limestone

Oolitic limestone

Fossilized shells

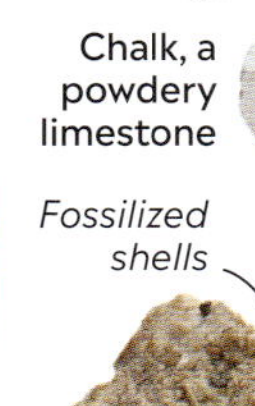

Shelly limestone

Sedimentary rocks
Rocks such as limestone and chalk form when sediment and the remains of sea creatures are buried and compacted.

Conglomerate, a sedimentary rock containing pebbles

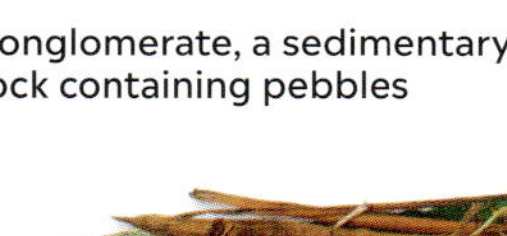

Plants – coal's raw ingredients

Ochre paint from clay

Red paint from hematite

Green paint from malachite

Blue paint from azurite

Yellow paint from orpiment

Pigments from rocks
Early people made paints by crushing coloured rocks or minerals and mixing the powder with animal fats.

Crystals
Sometimes, minerals form crystals with regular solid shapes and smooth external surfaces. Highly prized crystals are cut as gemstones.

Quartz crystals

Gemstones
Precious gemstones are rare, beautiful, and durable. Cutting and polishing reveals colour and sparkle.

Pink sapphire · Emerald · Aquamarine · Iridescent black opal · Yellow heliodor

Coloured diamonds

Diamonds
Diamond, the hardest of all known minerals, is famed for its brilliance.

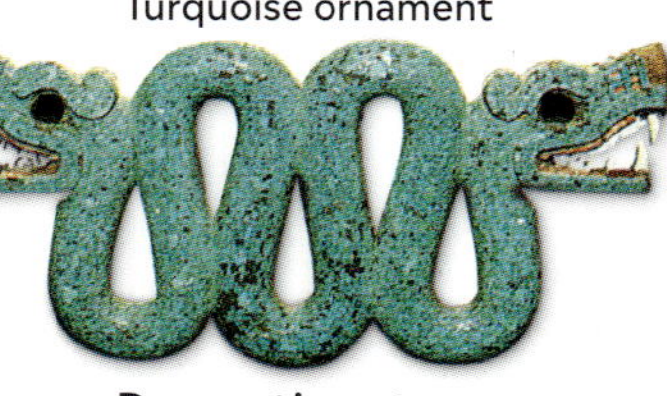

Turquoise ornament

Decorative stones
Colourful rocks and minerals, such as lapis lazuli and turquoise, have been used in decoration for thousands of years.

Schist

Slate

Unpolished marble

Metamorphic rocks
These rocks form when igneous or sedimentary rocks are altered by heat or pressure, or by both. Examples include marble, slate, and schist.

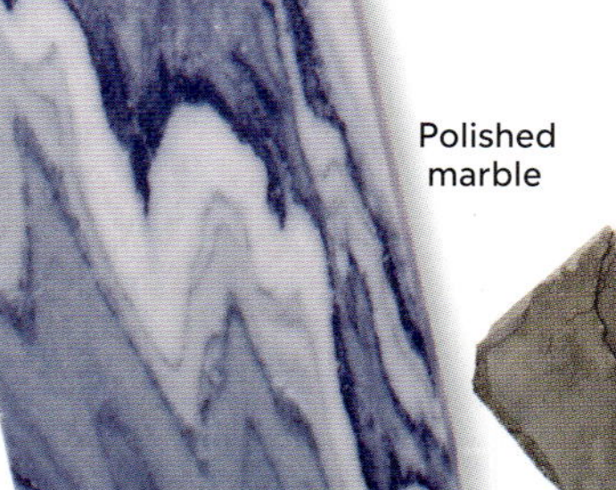

Polished marble

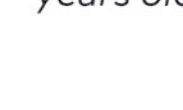

Welsh slate

Story of coal
Millions of years ago, plants that rotted on the damp forest floor were buried and compressed into peat. Further compression and heat formed lignite, then bituminous coal, then hard anthracite.

Peat

Lignite formed from compressed peat

Muddy rock

Preserved leaf, around 40 million years old

Fossils
Fossils are the remains of plants and animals preserved in sedimentary rocks, such as limestone.

Bituminous, household coal

Anthracite

Cave of the Crystals, Chihuahua, Mexico

CRYSTAL & GEM

Crystals are everywhere – in rocks, as salt in the kitchen, and even in bones. Crystalline minerals consist of atoms (small particles, including oxygen) and elements (such as iron). Gemstones are rare, well-formed crystals.

Orthoclase feldspar

Mica

Quartz

Crystals in rock

This graphite specimen has large crystals of the feldspar mineral orthoclase, with small crystals of quartz and biotite mica. Crystals without enough space grow irregularly.

Human arm bone

Organic crystals

Both animals and plants contain tiny crystals: Bones of vertebrate mammals (animals with backbones) are made up of the mineral apatite, and algae cell walls contain silica crystals.

Pan used to separate heavy minerals from river sediment

Searching for minerals

Minerals have been sought since prehistoric times. They can be plentiful, or scarce and more valuable. Some are extracted by quarrying from rock, and others by panning from rivers.

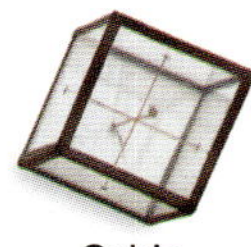

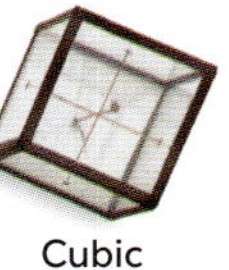

Triclinic model

Cubic model

Hexagonal model

Crystal systems

Crystals are classified into seven systems according to their shape and symmetry. These glass models, made in Germany around 1900, help us understand varied crystal shapes.

Hardness scale

A crystal can be identified by its properties, such as colour or hardness. In 1812, German mineralogist Friedrich Mohs devised a scale to test hardness.

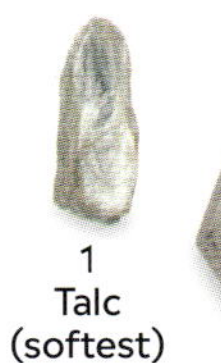

1 Talc (softest)

2 Gypsum

3 Calcite

4 Fluorite

5 Apatite

6 Orthoclase

7 Quartz

8 Topaz

9 Corundum

10 Diamond

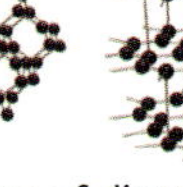

Structure of diamond (left) and graphite (right)

Graphite

Internal structure

Atomic structure determines crystal properties. Each carbon atom in a diamond is strongly bonded to four others. This rigid structure makes it exceptionally hard. Graphite's weakly bonded, widely spaced carbon atoms make it soft, between 1 and 2 on the Mohs scale.

Amethyst crystals

Amethyst crystals

These are the most prized form of quartz. The best crystals come from veins of granite in the Ural Mountains, Russia.

Azurite

Iridescent crystals

Hematite

Pink cobalt minerals

Erythrite

Sulfur

Crystal colours

A crystal's colour can be a striking feature: sulfur is bright yellow, azurite a rich blue, and hematite is iridescent (has rainbowlike colours). Cobalt is coloured by impurities.

Green emerald

Emerald crystals

Emerald is a variety of beryl, and is usually found in pegmatites and granites.

Crown jewels

The British Imperial State Crown has 2,868 diamonds, 273 pearls, 17 sapphires, 11 emeralds, and five rubies.

Sapphire

Diamonds

Black Prince's Ruby

Cullinan II diamond

Emerald

Benitoite

These blue crystals, found near the San Benito River, in California, US, are very rare. This many well-formed benitoite crystals have not been found anywhere else.

Benitoite crystals

Quartz crystals

Globular calcite crystals

Acicular mesolite crystals

Crystal habit

A crystal's shape is called its habit. Many crystals grow in aggregates (groups). Some aggregates are acicular (needlelike). Others are globular (spherical).

Calcite crystals can form as water drips from cave ceilings.

How crystals form

Crystals form as molten magma cools, or as liquid evaporates from a solution with a dissolved mineral. A crystal is built up from a lattice of atoms; each atom has its position and always bonds with others in the same way to form the mineral's crystals.

Quartz

Quartz crystals are made of silicon and oxygen atoms, forming a common mineral found in many rocks.

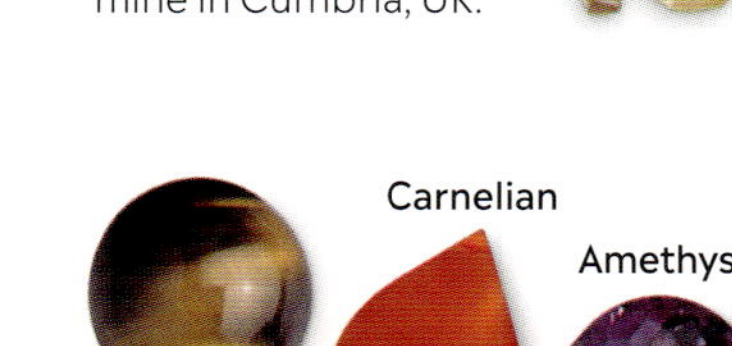

Barite

These golden-yellow barite crystals were produced by a 19th-century iron mine in Cumbria, UK.

Crystalline gold nugget

Gold, silver, and platinum are all crystalline, but it is rare to find single crystals. Named the Latrobe nugget, this rare cluster of gold crystals was discovered in 1855 in Victoria, Australia.

Ruby crystal

Ruby is a variety of the mineral corundum, an aluminium oxide. Only true red corundum stones are rubies. The finest rubies come from the Mogok region of Myanmar.

Crystal of ruby embedded in calcite

Coral in a warm sea

Tiger's-eye

Carnelian

Amethyst

Ruby

Opal

Sapphire Buddha

Emerald

Garnet

Chrysoberyl

Aquamarine

Topaz

Gemstones

Most gemstones are natural, inorganic crystals chosen for their beauty, durability, and rarity.

Jet, formed from ancient plant life

Natural gemstones

Organic gems (coral, jet, pearl) come from plants and animals, and are not as durable as inorganic gems.

Crystal healing

Some people believe crystals (usually quartz) have the ability to promote healing in the body.

Crystal timing

Quartz is piezoelectric. When an electric current passes through quartz, it vibrates regularly and can be used to keep time.

Special cuts

Rare stones may be given special cuts to keep them weighty, or unusual cuts for special occasions.

Heart-cut heliodor

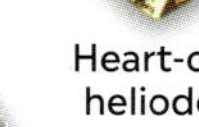

Irregular-cut sapphire

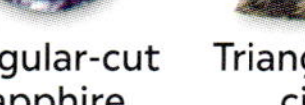

Triangular-cut citrine

Mother-of-pearl lining inside shell

A fossilized *Tyrannosaurus rex* skeleton

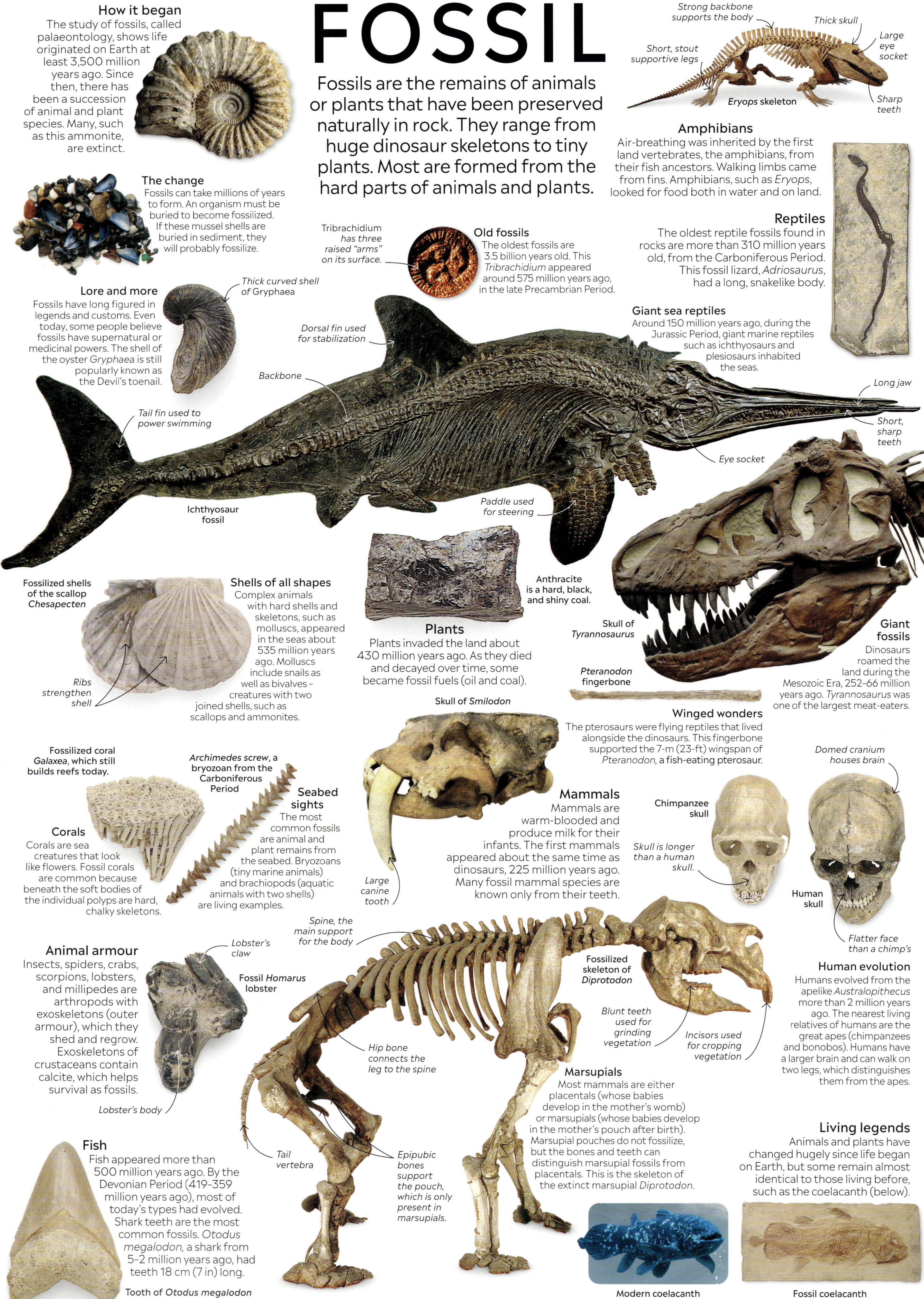

FOSSIL

Fossils are the remains of animals or plants that have been preserved naturally in rock. They range from huge dinosaur skeletons to tiny plants. Most are formed from the hard parts of animals and plants.

How it began

The study of fossils, called palaeontology, shows life originated on Earth at least 3,500 million years ago. Since then, there has been a succession of animal and plant species. Many, such as this ammonite, are extinct.

The change

Fossils can take millions of years to form. An organism must be buried to become fossilized. If these mussel shells are buried in sediment, they will probably fossilize.

Lore and more

Fossils have long figured in legends and customs. Even today, some people believe fossils have supernatural or medicinal powers. The shell of the oyster *Gryphaea* is still popularly known as the Devil's toenail.

Old fossils

The oldest fossils are 3.5 billion years old. This *Tribrachidium* appeared around 575 million years ago, in the late Precambrian Period.

Amphibians

Air-breathing was inherited by the first land vertebrates, the amphibians, from their fish ancestors. Walking limbs came from fins. Amphibians, such as *Eryops*, looked for food both in water and on land.

Reptiles

The oldest reptile fossils found in rocks are more than 310 million years old, from the Carboniferous Period. This fossil lizard, *Adriosaurus*, had a long, snakelike body.

Giant sea reptiles

Around 150 million years ago, during the Jurassic Period, giant marine reptiles such as ichthyosaurs and plesiosaurs inhabited the seas.

Shells of all shapes

Complex animals with hard shells and skeletons, such as molluscs, appeared in the seas about 535 million years ago. Molluscs include snails as well as bivalves – creatures with two joined shells, such as scallops and ammonites.

Plants

Plants invaded the land about 430 million years ago. As they died and decayed over time, some became fossil fuels (oil and coal).

Giant fossils

Dinosaurs roamed the land during the Mesozoic Era, 252–66 million years ago. *Tyrannosaurus* was one of the largest meat-eaters.

Winged wonders

The pterosaurs were flying reptiles that lived alongside the dinosaurs. This fingerbone supported the 7-m (23-ft) wingspan of *Pteranodon*, a fish-eating pterosaur.

Corals

Corals are sea creatures that look like flowers. Fossil corals are common because beneath the soft bodies of the individual polyps are hard, chalky skeletons.

Seabed sights

The most common fossils are animal and plant remains from the seabed. Bryozoans (tiny marine animals) and brachiopods (aquatic animals with two shells) are living examples.

Mammals

Mammals are warm-blooded and produce milk for their infants. The first mammals appeared about the same time as dinosaurs, 225 million years ago. Many fossil mammal species are known only from their teeth.

Animal armour

Insects, spiders, crabs, scorpions, lobsters, and millipedes are arthropods with exoskeletons (outer armour), which they shed and regrow. Exoskeletons of crustaceans contain calcite, which helps survival as fossils.

Human evolution

Humans evolved from the apelike *Australopithecus* more than 2 million years ago. The nearest living relatives of humans are the great apes (chimpanzees and bonobos). Humans have a larger brain and can walk on two legs, which distinguishes them from the apes.

Marsupials

Most mammals are either placentals (whose babies develop in the mother's womb) or marsupials (whose babies develop in the mother's pouch after birth). Marsupial pouches do not fossilize, but the bones and teeth can distinguish marsupial fossils from placentals. This is the skeleton of the extinct marsupial *Diprotodon*.

Fish

Fish appeared more than 500 million years ago. By the Devonian Period (419–359 million years ago), most of today's types had evolved. Shark teeth are the most common fossils. *Otodus megalodon*, a shark from 5–2 million years ago, had teeth 18 cm (7 in) long.

Living legends

Animals and plants have changed hugely since life began on Earth, but some remain almost identical to those living before, such as the coelacanth (below).

A volcanic eruption on Reykjanes Peninsula, Iceland

VOLCANO & EARTHQUAKE

Earth's crust is made up of many giant slabs of rock called tectonic plates. Most volcanoes and earthquakes occur where these plates collide, rub together, or move apart, resulting in potential damage to people and property.

Types of volcano

Volcanoes are of different shapes and sizes, depending on the thickness of their lava, how fast the lava cools, and the shape of their vents.

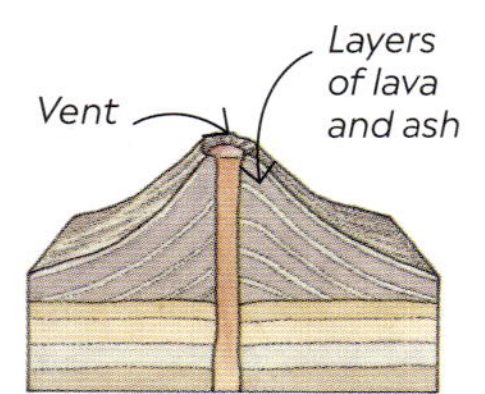

Ash and cinder volcano
Cone-shaped volcanoes form when magma erupts from a single vent, building up layers of lava and ash.

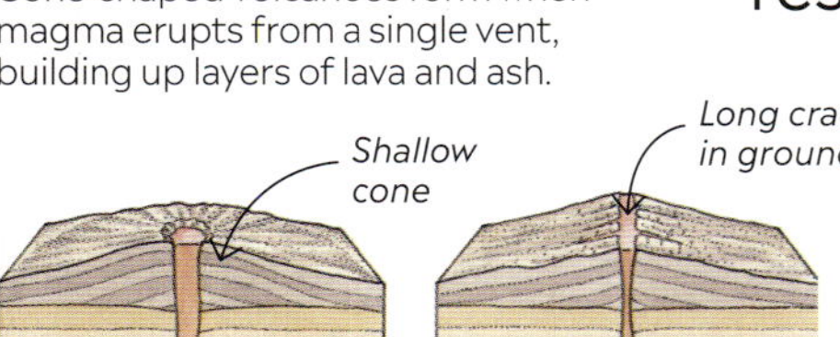

Shield volcano
Runny basalt lava flows out steadily to form this broad, gently sloping volcano.

Fissure volcano
This occurs where lava oozes through a long crack in the ground, often along ocean ridges.

Lava flows

The two main types of lava flows get their names from Hawaiian words. Aa (pronounced *ah-ah*) flows are covered in sharp, angular chunks of lava. Pahoehoe (*pa-hoy-hoy*) flows grow a skin over the hot, runny lava.

Pahoehoe flow
A hot pahoehoe flow bulges through a crack in its own skin. As it cools, new skin forms over the bulge. These flows cool into wrinkled mounds of rock.

Wrinkled skin looks like coils of rope.

Pahoehoe
This lava is more fluid than aa and contains more gas. The crust of a pahoehoe flow may grow up to 1 m (3 ft) thick.

Aa
This runny lava flows quickly in open channels, and its surface cools and hardens first. Further flows break the surface crust into rough blocks.

Volcanic eruption

Volcanoes erupt violently when the build-up of magma (molten rock) in the chamber below the vent creates enough pressure to blast through the vent.

A cloud of ash, gas, and rock fragments is hurled into the air.

Magma pouring out of the vent is called lava.

Side vent topped by a small cone

Trees will catch fire as lava arrives.

Volcanic slopes are formed by repeated lava flows.

Magma slowly forces its way up towards the surface.

Magma collects in the magma chamber, increasing pressure on the clogged vent.

Cone built up from successive layers of lava and ash

Hot, gassy, molten rock (magma) rises from deep inside Earth.

Volcanic phases

Volcanoes can be active, extinct, or dormant (sleeping).

Active
Every year, around 25 major volcanic eruptions occur on land.

Extinct
These are volcanoes that have stopped erupting altogether.

Pyroclastic debris

Volcanoes blast out millions of rock fragments called pyroclasts. These fragments range from house-sized blocks to fine, powdery dust.

Tephra
This is ash and chunks of pyroclastic rock blasted out of a volcano.

Volcanic bombs
These are rounded chunks of rock thrown out from a volcano.

Lapilli
Lapilli (Latin for "little stones") are chunks of frothy lava containing air bubbles.

Pele's hair
In Hawaii, fluid lava forms strands called Pele's hair (after the Hawaiian goddess of volcanoes).

Eruption of Vesuvius

In 79 CE, Mount Vesuvius, a volcano near Naples, Italy, erupted violently, killing thousands of people living in the nearby towns of Pompeii and Herculaneum.

Plastercast bodies
Ash set around the bodies of dying Pompeiians like wet cement. Plastercasts made of the bodies show how they died.

Cast of mother and child from Pompeii

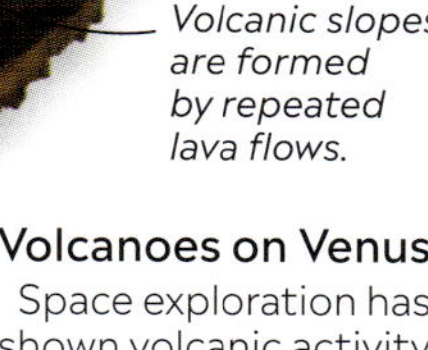

Volcanoes on Venus

Space exploration has shown volcanic activity on other planets in the Solar System. Images of Venus's surface, taken by the spacecraft *Magellan* in the early 1990s, reveal huge volcanoes and craters.

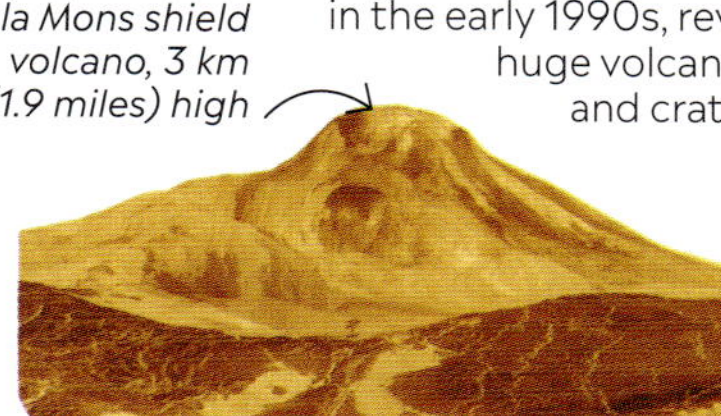

Gula Mons shield volcano, 3 km (1.9 miles) high

Geysers

These occur in volcanic areas, where water heated by magma underground bursts out through a vent or crack as jets of water and steam.

Earthquakes

Like volcanoes, many earthquakes occur where Earth's tectonic plates meet. Most are too small to be felt, but some shake the ground violently and destroy whole cities.

Seismograms
These are printed records of the shock waves from an earthquake recorded on a seismograph.

Height of the lines indicate shock waves' intensity.

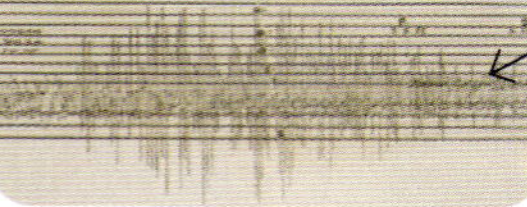

Seismogram of the 1923 Tokyo earthquake

Seismographs
The power of a quake can be recorded by a seismograph. The first seismograph (part of which is shown on the left) was invented by Italian scientist Luigi Palmieri in 1856.

Thermal imaging camera
This device can detect the heat of a living person, and is used to find people trapped in rubble after an earthquake.

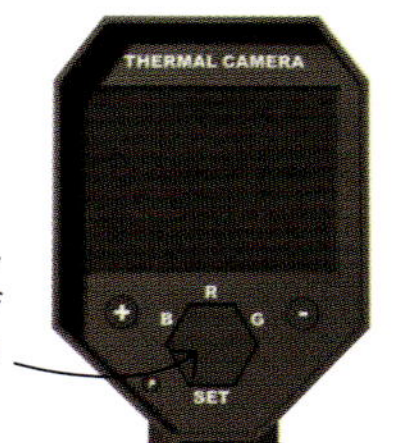

Control for showing level of infrared radiation

Earthquake damage
This building in Taiwan slipped off its foundation and partially collapsed during an earthquake in 2018. Most earthquakes last just a few minutes, but can still be destructive.

A supercell thunderstorm

WEATHER

Wind, rain, snow, fog, frost, and sunshine are all signs of the constant shifting of Earth's atmosphere. The weather changes in four main ways – movement, temperature, moisture content, and pressure.

Seaweed strands shrivel in fine weather, and swell and feel damp if rain threatens.

Wet

Dry

Natural signs

The natural world can provide useful clues about the weather to come. A pine cone is one of the most reliable weather indicators. In dry weather, the scales open out. When they close, it is a good sign that rain is on the way.

Catching the wind

The wind is simply air in motion. It can move slowly, giving a gentle breeze, or rapidly, creating gales and hurricanes. Wind direction can be indicated by weather vanes or by pennants (flags) flown on ships.

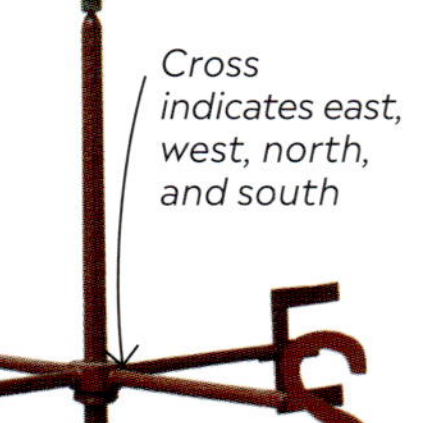

Head indicates the direction the wind is coming from.

Cross indicates east, west, north, and south

Ship's pennant

Weather vane

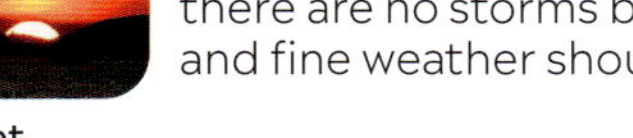

Sunrise

Sunset

Message in the sky

In the northern hemisphere, where the weather tends to blow from the west, a red sky in the morning indicates that the Sun is casting its rays on storm clouds from the west. A red sky as the Sun sets in the west means there are no storms blowing in, and fine weather should follow.

Cloud watching

Clouds float across the sky in all sorts of shapes, sizes, and colours. There are three main types: cirrus (wispy), cumulus (heaped), and stratus (layered). Other clouds are mixtures of these three types. Clouds are made of ice or water, depending on their height above ground.

Digital anemometer

This handheld device is used to measure wind speed, providing readings to a high level of accuracy. Anemometers are used at weather stations to study weather patterns.

Cirrus

Cirrus clouds (left) form high in the troposphere (the lowest layer of the atmosphere). It is so cold here that the clouds are made entirely from ice crystals. Strong winds blow the crystals into wispy strands, sometimes called "mares' tails".

Pen draws lines on revolving graph paper.

Barometer

This aneroid barometer records changes in air pressure. As the air pressure changes, the cylindrical drum expands and contracts, and a pen draws the ups and downs on the rotating graph paper. A change in air pressure brings a change in the weather.

Flying eye

Equipment on a weather forecasting plane monitors all sorts of weather conditions and measures temperature and humidity high in the atmosphere.

Cirrostratus

Cirrostratus clouds (right) are sheetlike, high-level clouds that occur when cirrus clouds spread out into thin, milky layers. The clouds can cover the whole sky. They usually appear 12–24 hours before rain or snow.

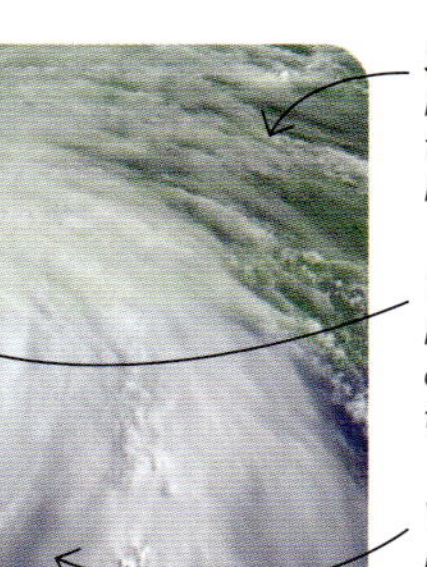

Spiral bands of rain surround the eye of the hurricane.

The eye of the hurricane is a calm area in the centre.

Whirling winds may reach speeds of up to 260 kph (200 mph).

Eye of a storm

This satellite image shows the swirling clouds of a hurricane as it approaches land. Weather forecasters use satellite images to plot wind speed and direction. They also gather information (such as temperature, rainfall, and changes in air pressure) from weather stations across the globe. The data is fed into supercomputers, which predict how weather systems will develop.

Cirrocumulus

Cirrocumulus (left) are tiny clumps of cloud containing ice crystals. This type of cloud make a pattern in the sky, known as a "mackerel sky". They often form ahead of stormy weather.

Mists and fog

When the wind is light, the sky clear, and the air damp, moisture in the air turns into water droplets near the ground, forming fog.

Morning dew

Sparkling dewdrops form when the cool night air cannot hold any more moisture, and condenses into tiny droplets.

Frost and ice

When temperatures plummet on a cold, dry winter's night, frost (white ice crystals) forms on cold surfaces, such as soil and trees.

Altocumulus

Altocumulus (right) are heaped masses of cloud, visible at mid-altitudes. They are usually white or grey, and often occur in sheets or patches with rounded edges. If they appear on a warm and humid morning, they may signal thunderstorms.

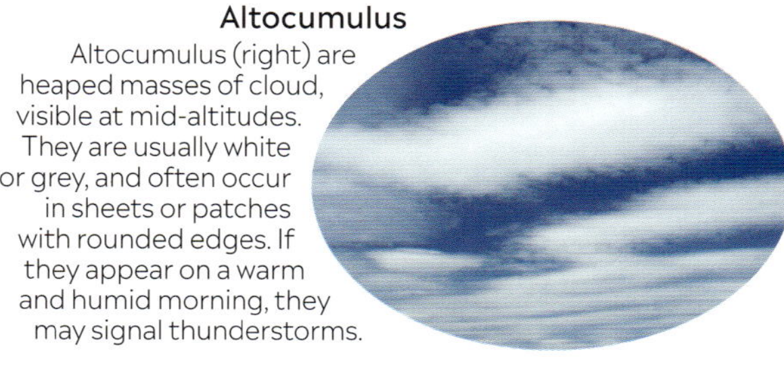

Thunderstorms

Inside thunderclouds, ice crystals and water collide, producing tiny electric charges. The base of the cloud is negatively charged, while the top of the cloud and the ground are positively charged. When the difference between the charges gets too great, the energy is discharged as lightning.

Stratocumulus

Stratocumulus clouds (left) form in rounded, bumpy layers, often with breaks of sky in between. They vary in colour from light to dark grey, and are often accompanied by weak rain.

Sunny day

In summer, sunny days tend to be hot, as there is little cloud to block out the Sun's rays.

Rainy day

Dark grey clouds signal rain. In heavy downpours, raindrops can be up to 5 mm (0.2 in) wide.

Rainbow

Rainbows form when sunlight is refracted (bent and split) by raindrops, creating a coloured arc.

Cumulus

Fluffy cumulus clouds (right) are formed when bubbles of warm air rise from Earth's surface. Water vapour in the air cools and condenses, forming cloud droplets. They usually last between 5 to 40 minutes.

Tornadoes

Tornadoes are masses of rising warm air, set spinning by high winds. Air pressure at the centre is so low, the air rushes into the funnel at enormous speed, sucking up everything in its path.

Drought

A drought is an abnormally long dry period, when there is below-average rainfall in a particular region.

Stratus

Stratus clouds (left) build up in flat, grey layers. They form as warm air rides slowly over cold air, and the moisture condenses from the air as it cools. This creates a vast blanket of cloud.

Monsoon

In the summer, monsoon winds bring heavy rain to subtropical regions. In winter, they bring drier, cooler weather. Although the monsoon brings rain after a long, dry season, the heavy rains often cause widespread flooding.

A tornado in Minnesota, US

HURRICANE & TORNADO

Ancient ideas
About 2,400 years ago, Greek philosophers Aristotle (right) and Plato (left) were among the first to try to explain scientifically how the weather works.

There are many forms of severe weather, such as hurricanes, tornadoes, droughts, heat waves, floods, and snowstorms. At their worst, these can be unpredictable and dangerous, resulting in casualties and damage to property, crops, and livelihoods.

Watching the sky
Legend describes how Tawhaki, the Maori god of thunder, disguised himself as a kite. Maori priests tried to predict the weather by watching how kites moved in the sky.

Maori kite made of canvas and twigs

Watching weather
Weather balloons carry instruments high in the sky that transmit back readings to Earth. This data helps in weather forecasting.

Wind recorder
This anemometer records wind speed and direction over time. To understand how the wind works, forecasters must take multiple measurements.

Cups spin around, blown by the wind.

Average wind speed is recorded as the cylinder rotates

Radar dish

Measuring tornadoes
A Doppler radar mounted on a truck measures wind speed in a tornado. Microwaves directed at a tornado bounce off water droplets carried by the wind. Computers in the truck work out how fast the droplets are moving by analysing the microwaves received at the radar dish.

Thunderstorms
When warm, moist air rises and cools, creating a huge thundercloud, the rising current of air may travel at more than 100 kph (60 mph). A lot of energy is released in strong winds, torrential rain, thunder, and lightning.

Deadly droughts
Large areas of land with no plants soon suffer from drought. Plants protect against winds, which can increase evaporation, and are stores of water, which binds together grains of soil. Dry mud cracks and goes brittle.

Tornado tales
Tornadoes are high-spiralling, fast-moving winds that leave behind a trail of destruction. They are also called whirlwinds or twisters.

Swirling black thundercloud

Average tornado travels along the ground for 8 km (5 miles).

Emergency food supplies

Disaster relief
When a natural disaster strikes a remote area, the quickest way to bring aid is to drop supplies from the sky. The food parcels supplied by this plane contained grain and cereals, which helped many stay alive during a drought in South Sudan.

Gusty winds
Hurricanes and other high winds are caused by huge differences in atmospheric pressure. As the air spirals inwards, it speeds up. This image shows Hurricane Wilma in Mexico, in 2005.

Each hump stores fat.

Bactrian camel, from Asia

Nature's survivors
Like many other animals that live in the constant drought of the desert, the camel can make water from its own body fat. It can use a quarter of its body weight to survive for weeks without fresh water.

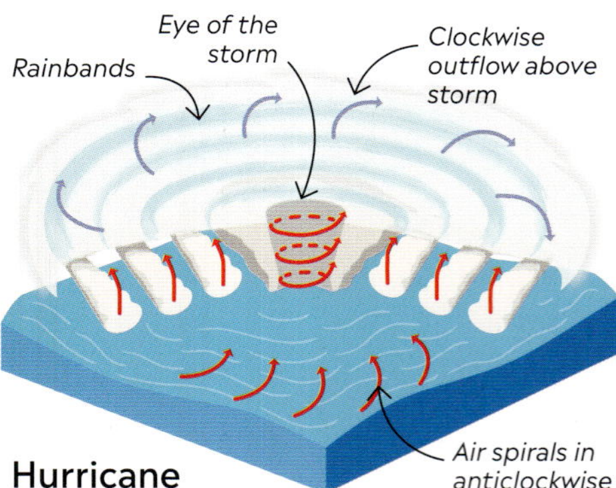

Hurricane development
Above warm oceans, moist, rising air leaves an area of very low pressure. Surrounding air spirals inwards, then air from the eye (centre) flows out above the storm in the opposite direction.

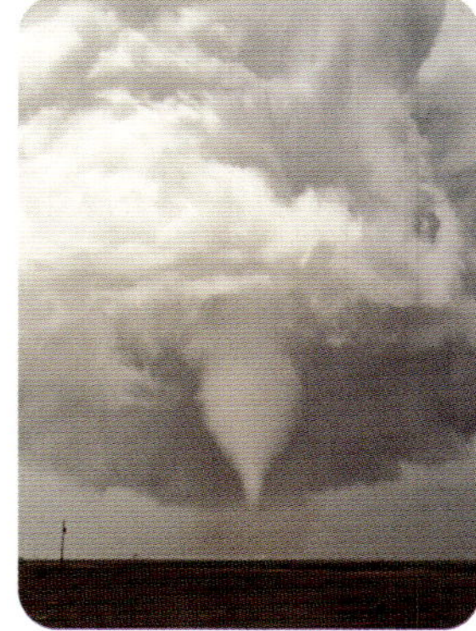

1. A cloud wall
The tornado's funnel descends from a thundercloud. A column of cloud forms as moisture in the air condenses in the low pressure inside the tornado.

2. Touching the ground
When the tornado meets the ground, its funnel is obscured by dust picked up by rising air and swirling winds. Its winds throw debris into the air.

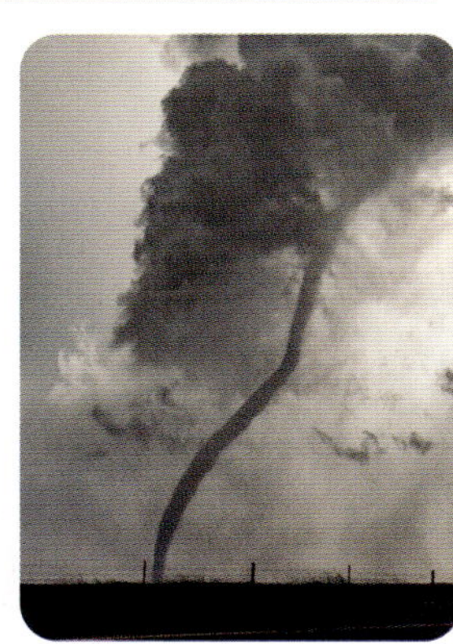

3. Losing power
As the tornado loses energy, it slows down and its funnel narrows. Eventually, the funnel loses its shape and shrinks back to the thundercloud.

Climate change
The world's average temperature is rising slowly – this is called global warming. If this continues, dense ice in the polar regions, such as the Hubbard Glacier in Alaska, US, will melt and cause sea levels to rise.

An avalanche in the Hindu Kush mountains, South and Central Asia

NATURAL DISASTERS

In addition to providing us with air, food, water, and warmth to survive, Earth also generates natural disasters. Some may be sudden, such as an earthquake, tornado, or flood. Others, such as a drought or the spread of a deadly disease, may occur gradually. Some of these are expected to increase in frequency and magnitude due to climate change.

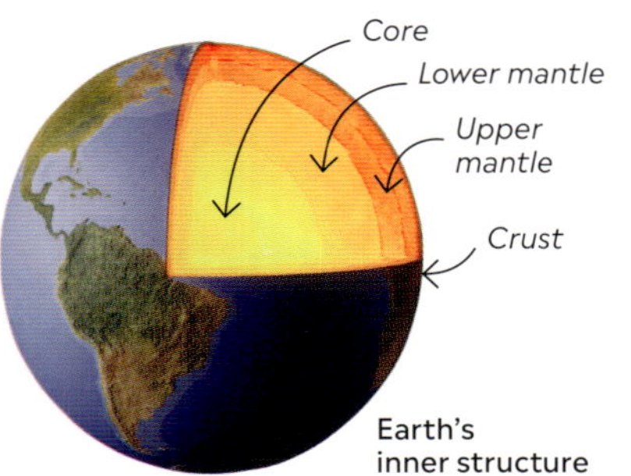

Earth's inner structure

Restless Earth

The heat from Earth's core drives movement in the mantle. Earth's crust is split into tectonic plates, which get slowly dragged around Earth's surface by the mantle. The crust is constantly renewed as the plates move, causing Earth's surface to change over time.

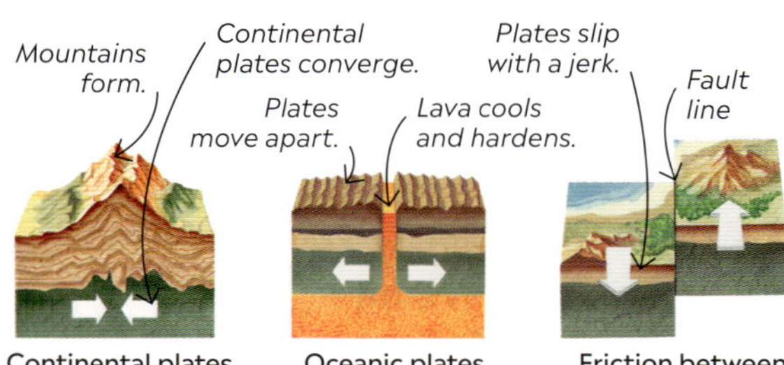

Continental plates converge to form mountains.

Oceanic plates diverge and molten lava creates new crust.

Friction between tectonic plates causes earthquakes.

On shaky ground

Although Earth's surface feels solid, its plates are moving all the time – sometimes gently, sometimes with a jolt. These movements are known as earthquakes.

Earthquake in Haiti

The strength, or magnitude, of earthquakes is measured by the Richter scale. A quake measuring 7 hit Haiti (right) on 12 January 2010, damaging 250,000 houses and killing 100,000 people.

Women queue to collect water in a flood in Bangladesh.

Tsunami

These massive, destructive waves, usually caused by undersea earthquakes, travel at up to 950 kph (590 mph) and may be as high as 30 m (98 ft) when they reach land. Here, a tsunami is overwhelming the coast defences of Miyako, a fishing port in Japan.

Floods

When storm waves sweep in from the sea, or a river floods after heavy rain or snow melt, settlements near coasts or banks may be swept away. Following a flood, water contamination can spread infections.

Landslides

When gravity overcomes the forces that hold soil and rock on a slope, loose material crashes down in a landslide. It may be triggered by heavy rains, erosion, or an earthquake, and can bury buildings and people, gathering force on its way down.

Mudslide rips through a Swiss mountain village.

Mighty volcanoes

As pressure builds up inside Earth, magma (hot, molten rock under the crust) and gas escape through a vent in its surface. This vent is a volcano and can pour out lava, ash, rocks, and toxic gases that can kill people and transform the landscape.

When magma erupts out of a volcano, it's called lava.

Pyroclastic flow from Mount Pinatubo in the Philippines

Pyroclastic flow

A volcanic eruption can send a column of rock particles, ash, and hot gases into the sky. If that column collapses, a deadly cloud of hot material, called a pyroclastic flow, engulfs the area.

Wild weather

The massive electrical charge of a lightning bolt in a thunderstorm can kill a person instantly. Aeroplanes like this WC-130J Hercules monitor storms by flying into them. The data gathered helps meteorologists to predict the weather and issue storm warnings.

Tornadoes

Tornadoes are the most violent storms and can travel at 200 kph (125 mph) with 500-kph (300-mph) winds. They can flatten everything in their path.

A swirling tornado in the American Midwest

Hurricane force

Hurricane Katrina hit the southern coast of the US in 2005. It killed 1,833 people and left millions homeless. This satellite image shows it moving over the Gulf of Mexico.

Fire engines are important in fighting wildfires

Fighting fires

In extremely dry weather, a wildfire may spread quickly and engulf entire forests. It may take a week for firefighters to bring it under control.

Pandemic

In 2019, a flu-like virus named coronavirus (COVID-19) was identified. It was declared a pandemic in March 2020 as it spread rapidly across the world. Scientists worked urgently to develop COVID-19 vaccines.

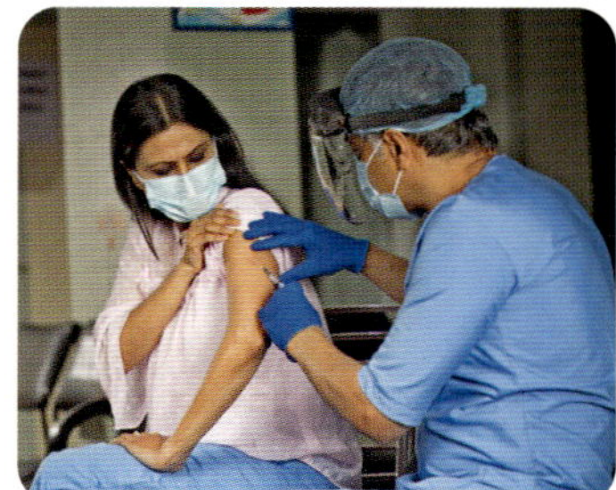

Infectious diseases

Diseases such as malaria and cholera have killed more people than any other natural disaster. They are caused by bacteria, fungi, and viruses. Some invade our bodies through mosquito bites.

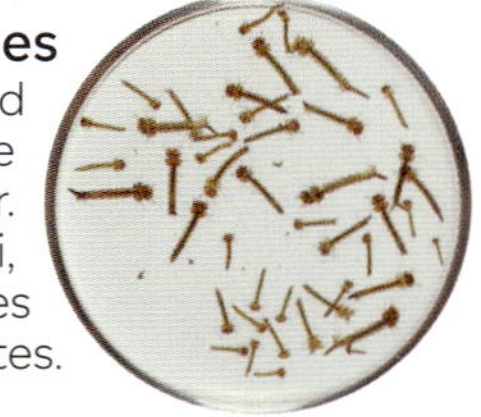

Mosquito larvae hatch into flying adults that spread malaria and dengue fever.

A 3.2-m (10.5-ft) infrared telescope near the Mauna Kea summit in Hawaii, US

Future disasters

Some people fear that a huge volcanic eruption, a mega-tsunami, or a collision with a Near Earth Object (NEO) could trigger a global climate disaster and end human civilization. Scientists use powerful telescopes to track comets and other NEOs.

Iguazú Falls, South America

WONDERS OF THE WORLD

From breathtaking natural wonders to history's finest examples of art, architecture, and engineering, the wonders of our world tell the story of planet Earth and all humankind.

Great Barrier Reef
The world's largest coral reef system stretches 2,600 km (1,600 miles) over a part of the Coral Sea in Australia.

Mount Everest
Earth's highest mountain, Mount Everest is situated in the Eastern Himalayas. It soars to 8,848 m (29,029 ft) above sea level.

Mount Fuji
At a height of 3,776 m (12,388 ft), Mount Fuji is a volcano as well as the highest mountain in Japan. It is famous for its beauty and is home to many Shinto shrines near its base.

The Dead Sea
At 427 m (1,400 ft) below sea level, the shores of the Dead Sea in Jordan and Israel mark Earth's lowest point on land. The lake is also one of the saltiest bodies of water.

The Grand Canyon
One of North America's most magnificent landscapes, the Grand Canyon is a valley that has been carved into the Colorado Plateau by the Colorado River over millions of years. It is known for its dramatic rock formations.

Cave of Crystals
Located in the Naica Mine in Mexico, this cave is filled with the largest natural crystals ever found. Made of the mineral gypsum, the largest crystal is 12 m (39 ft) long.

Salar de Uyuni
Once a prehistoric lake, Bolivia's Salar de Uyuni is the world's largest salt flat. It covers an area of 10,582 sq km (4,086 sq miles), and is the flattest place on Earth.

The Namib Desert
This immense desert extends for about 2,000 km (1,243 miles) along the coast of southwest Africa. The dunes in this desert are some of the highest in the world.

Stonehenge
A circle of massive standing stones known as Stonehenge stands in Salisbury Plain in the south of England. It is one of the world's most famous Stone Age structures, and was built around 2,500 BCE.

Moai statues
Between the 11th and 17th centuries, the Rapa Nui people carved around 900 statues, called *moai*, on the island of Rapa Nui (Easter Island) in the Pacific.

The pyramids of Giza
Situated on the banks of the River Nile in Egypt, the pyramids at Giza include the Great Pyramid. One of the Seven Wonders of the Ancient World, it was built around 2,500 BCE.

Angkor Wat
This 12th-century temple complex in Cambodia is an example of Khmer art and architecture. It is the world's largest religious structure.

Machu Picchu
This Inca citadel and temple complex sits high on a mountain ridge in Peru. It was founded by the Inca ruler Pachacuti Inca Yupanqui in the 15th century. The structures of Machu Picchu are made from blocks of granite and arranged to withstand earthquakes.

The Great Wall of China
This series of walls, built between the 3rd century BCE and the 17th century CE, is the longest human-made structure. It spans more than 20,000 km (12,400 miles).

Petra
Petra in Jordan was a prosperous trading city about 2,000 years ago. It includes striking architecture including the famous Al-Khazneh.

The Colosseum
The largest Roman amphitheatre, the Colosseum was built in the 1st century CE. It was designed to hold about 50,000 people.

Burj Khalifa
The world's tallest building, the Burj Khalifa in Dubai, UAE, reaches a height of more than 828 m (2,716 ft). It was built between 2004 and 2009.

Bismuth crystals

PERIODIC TABLE

The periodic table is a chart that lists all of the 118 known elements, along with key information about them. The table is "periodic", or repeating, because the characteristics of elements follow a pattern.

Elemental information

The atomic number is equal to the number of protons in the nucleus of an atom of this element.

A symbol is a shortened form of the element's name.

The full name is given for every element.

The atomic mass number is the average atomic mass of all the atoms of the element. The atomic mass is equal to the total number of protons and neutrons in an atom. For some radioactive elements, their atomic mass numbers are shown in brackets. These numbers belong to their most stable forms.

Each element is represented by a tile, which contains its full name, symbol, and atomic number (from 1 to 118). An image and the atomic mass number are also included.

Clear glass spheres contain invisible gases.

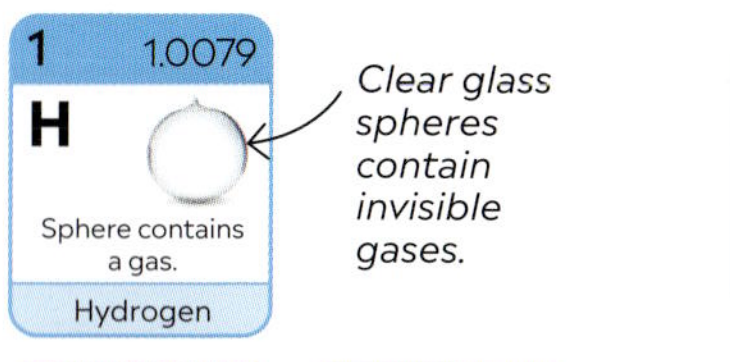
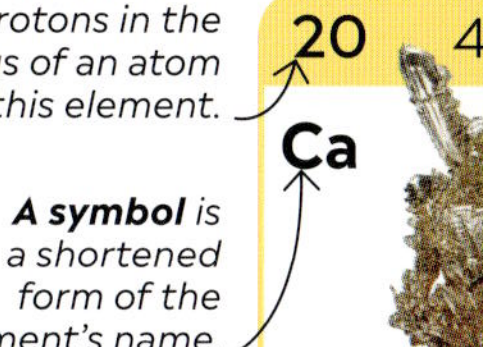
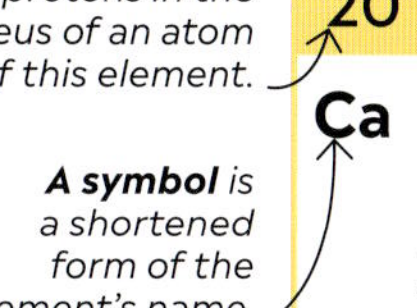
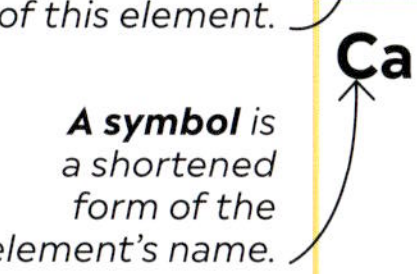
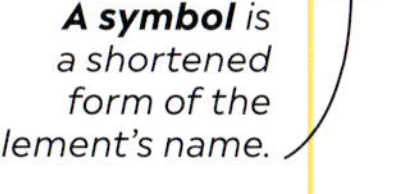
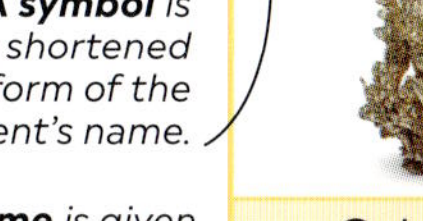
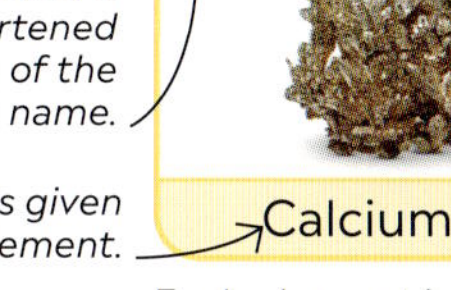
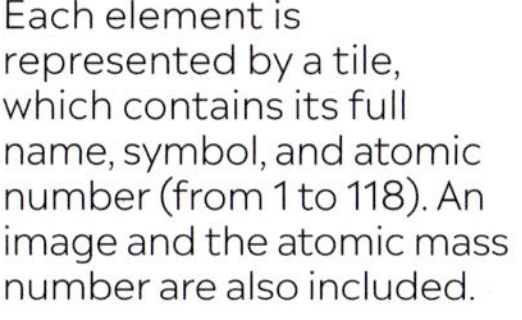
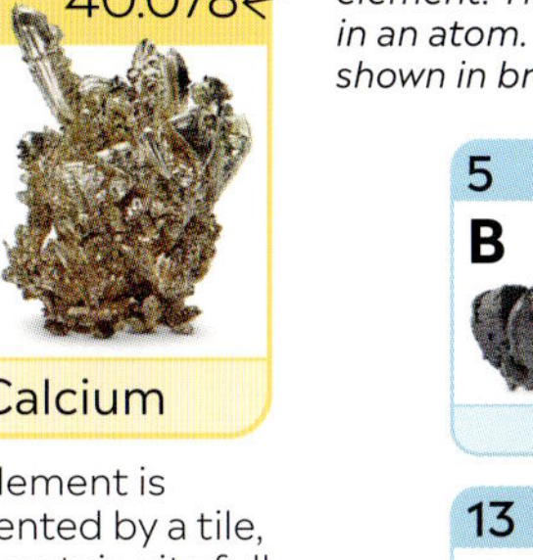
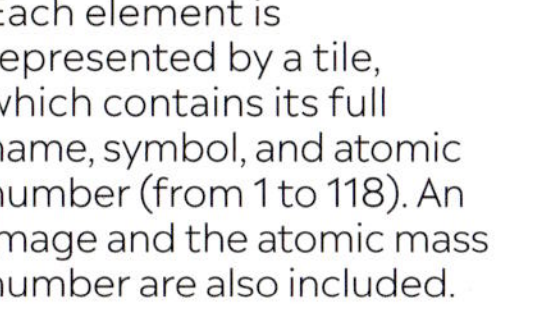
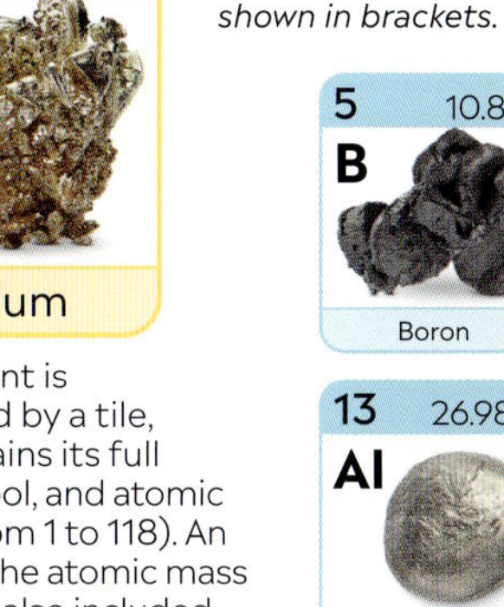
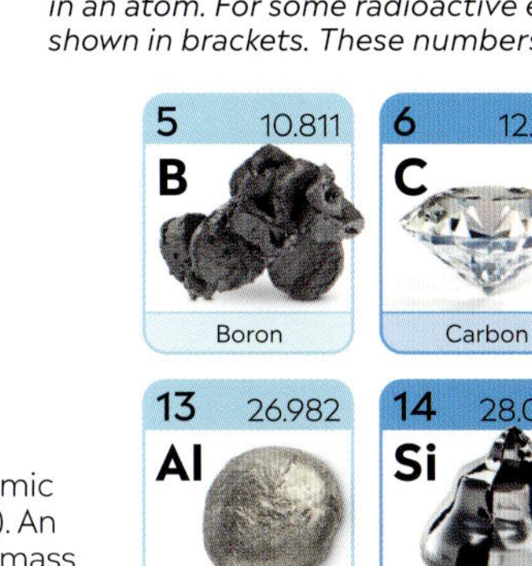
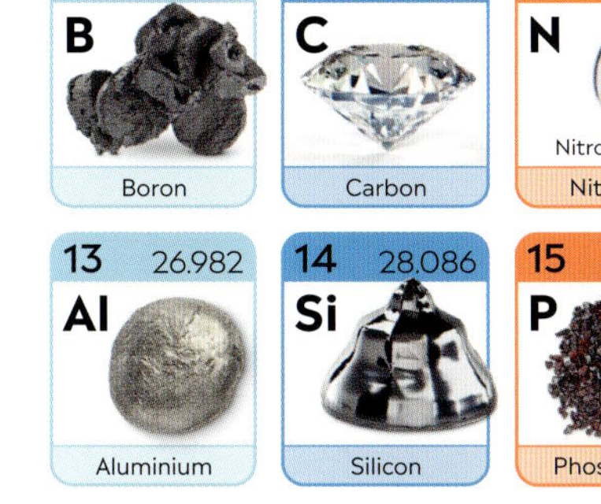

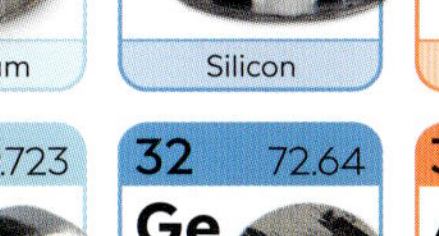
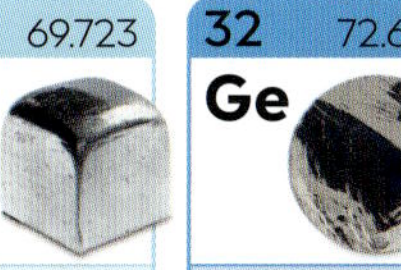

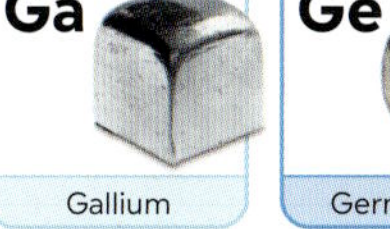
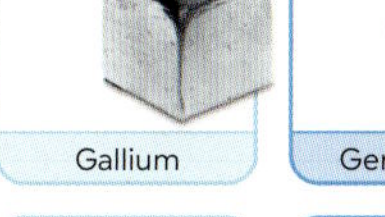
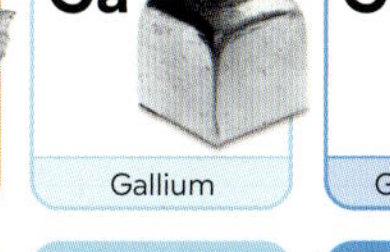
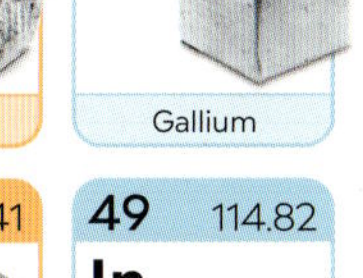
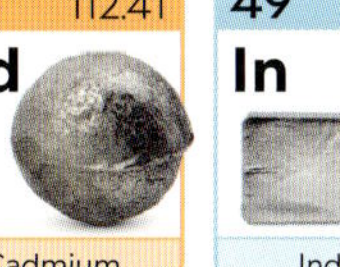

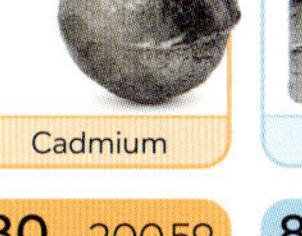
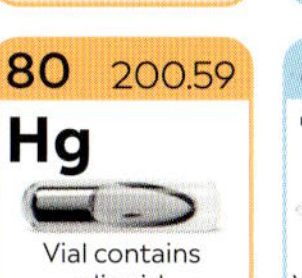
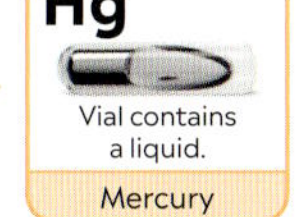
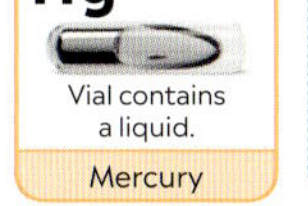

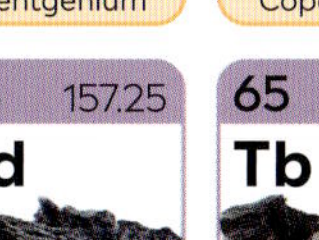

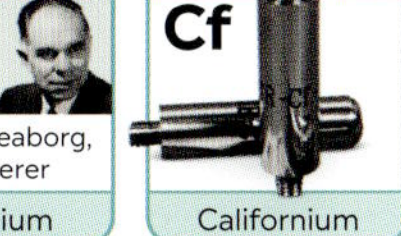

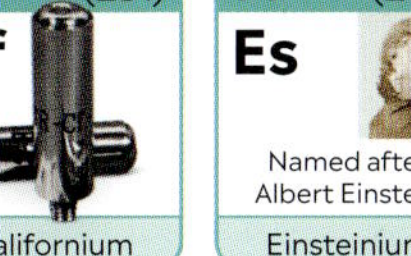
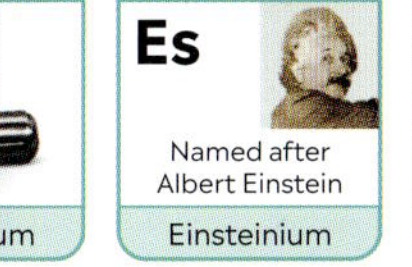

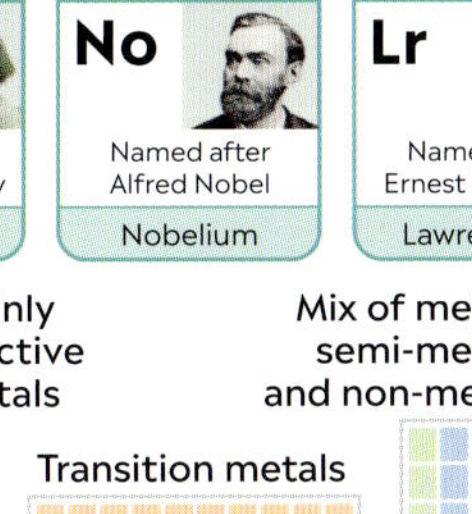

Inside an atom

Atoms, the smallest units of an element, are made up of even smaller "subatomic" particles called protons, electrons, and neutrons. Neutrons and protons are found in the nucleus at the centre of the atom, while electrons orbit the nucleus. The number of protons in an atom of an element is unique to that element.

KEY

- Hydrogen
- Alkali Metals
- Alkaline Earth Metals
- Transition Metals
- Lanthanides
- Actinides
- The Boron Group
- The Carbon Group
- The Nitrogen Group
- The Oxygen Group
- Halogens
- Noble Gases

Groups

Vertical columns are called groups. The elements here have similar chemical properties. Atoms of the elements get bigger as you move down the group.

Groups run from top to bottom.

Periods

Horizontal rows are called periods. From left to right, atoms across a period increase in mass.

Periods run from left to right.

Blocks

A block is a larger collection of elements. The table is divided into four blocks – "s" block (mainly reactive metals), "d" block (transition metals), "p" block (metals, semi-metals, and non-metals), and "f" block (lanthanides and actinides).

Mainly reactive metals

Transition metals

Mix of metals, semi-metals, and non-metals

Lanthanides and actinides

Jupiter's southern hemisphere captured by NASA's spacecraft Juno

PLANETS

Our Solar System has eight planets. A planet is a body orbiting the Sun, massive enough for its gravity to make it nearly round and to have cleared other objects out of its orbit.

The Sun

A ball of hot, luminous gas, the Sun is the largest member of the Solar System, and its gravity holds the system together. The energy released from the Sun fuels life on Earth.

Rocky planets

Mercury, Venus, Earth, and Mars are all balls of rock and metal, but are very different on the surface. Earth has life and oceans, Mars is a frozen desert, Venus has a volcanic surface, and Mercury is covered with craters. They are the Solar System's smallest planets.

Mercury

Mercury is the smallest, and closest to the Sun. Its thin atmosphere cannot retain heat, and it is freezing at night.

Venus

Venus has the hottest surface temperature of all the planets. It is covered with lava plains and extinct volcanoes.

Earth

Earth is the largest of the inner planets. The water on its surface makes it appear blue from space.

Mars

The Red Planet is the coldest of the rocky planets. It has the biggest volcanoes and canyons.

Exploring the rocky planets

Spacecraft have visited all rocky planets, but Mars is the most visited. The robotic, car-sized rover Curiosity landed in 2012 and has sent us vivid images of Mars's terrain.

Solar System

The planets orbit the Sun at the centre of the Solar System. They travel in a disclike plane, occupying a region that extends about 4.5 billion km (2.8 billion miles) out from the Sun.

Giant planets

Jupiter, Saturn, Uranus, and Neptune are the outermost and largest planets. Jupiter and Saturn are mostly composed of lightweight hydrogen. Uranus and Neptune contain water and other chemicals in an icy slush. Each giant is wrapped in a deep atmosphere with complex clouds. All have ring systems.

What are planets made of?

The rocky planets have a metal core surrounded by a layer of rock called the mantle. The giants have thick atmospheres of mainly hydrogen, rather than solid surfaces. These surround liquid-like layers, and each giant planet is thought to have a core of denser materials.

Jupiter

Jupiter is the Solar System's most massive planet. Rapid rotation, fierce winds, and large-scale movement of gases create the bands in its atmosphere.

Uranus

This ice giant (below) is encircled by faint, dark rings. It spins on its side and takes 84 years to complete a single orbit of the Sun.

Saturn

The second-largest of the planets has a wide system of rings. Like Jupiter, Saturn is made of mainly hydrogen and helium, but has less than a third of Jupiter's matter.

Neptune

Neptune is also an ice giant – made of mainly water, ammonia, and methane. It has a long orbit, taking 165 years to circle the Sun.

Minor members

The Asteroid Belt, and the Kuiper Belt far beyond Neptune, contain countless rock and ice-and-rock bodies. The largest of these minor members are the dwarf planets, such as Pluto (front right, with its moon Charon).

Exploring the Kuiper Belt

The spacecraft New Horizons flew by Pluto on 14 July 2015, sending back hundreds of images. In 2019, it flew past the small Kuiper Belt Object Arrokoth.

Exploring the giant planets

The first spacecraft to venture beyond the rocky planets were Pioneer 10 and 11 and Voyager 1 and 2. Juno (left) went into orbit around Jupiter in 2016.

Explorers on the Moon

Six Apollo missions took 12 men to the Moon between 1969 and 1972. Space agencies are now aiming to take crewed missions to Mars by 2040.

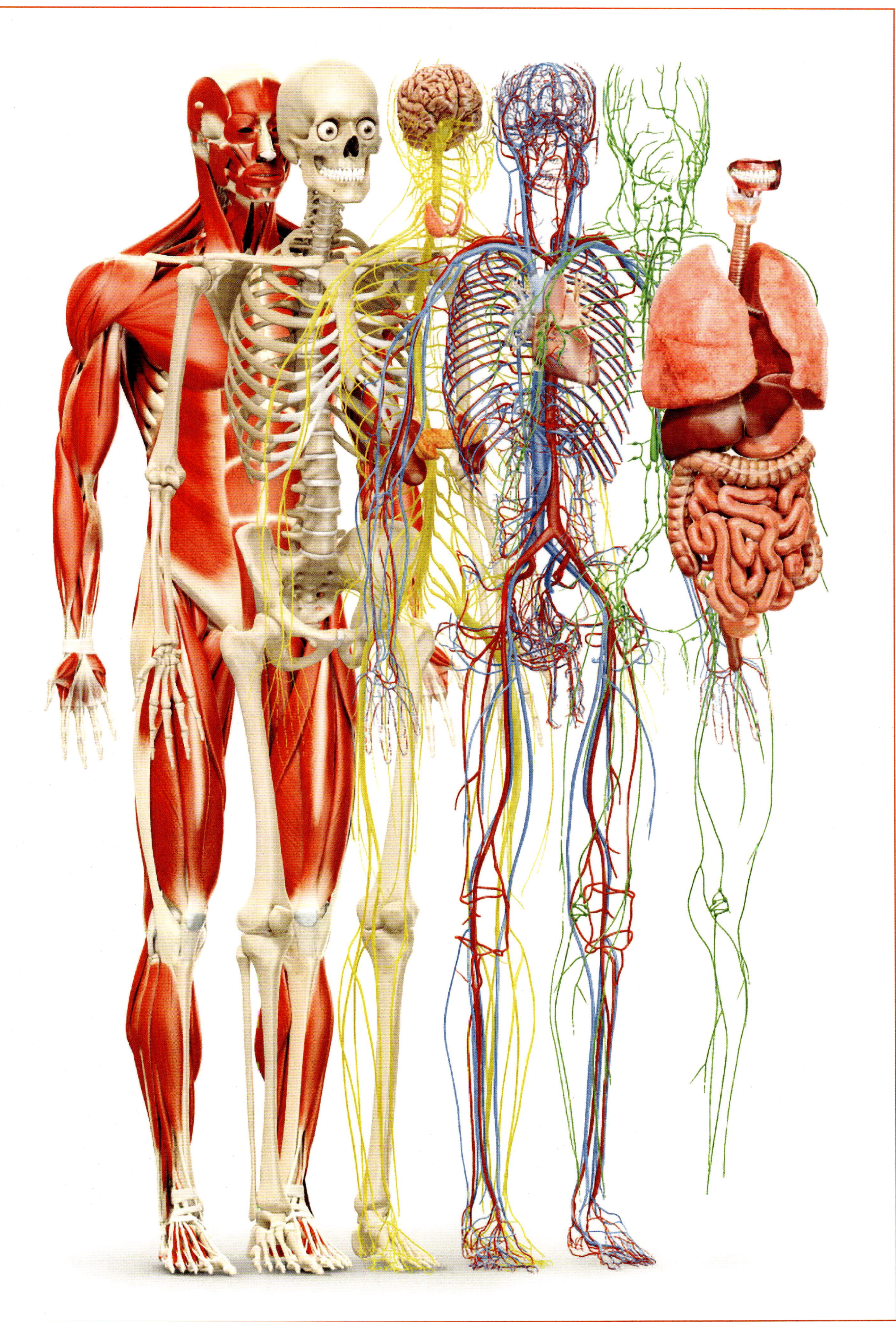

The different systems of the human body

HUMAN BODY

The human body is made up from 12 major systems, including the skeletal, muscular, digestive, and nervous systems. Together, these systems enable us to move, talk, and perceive the world around us.

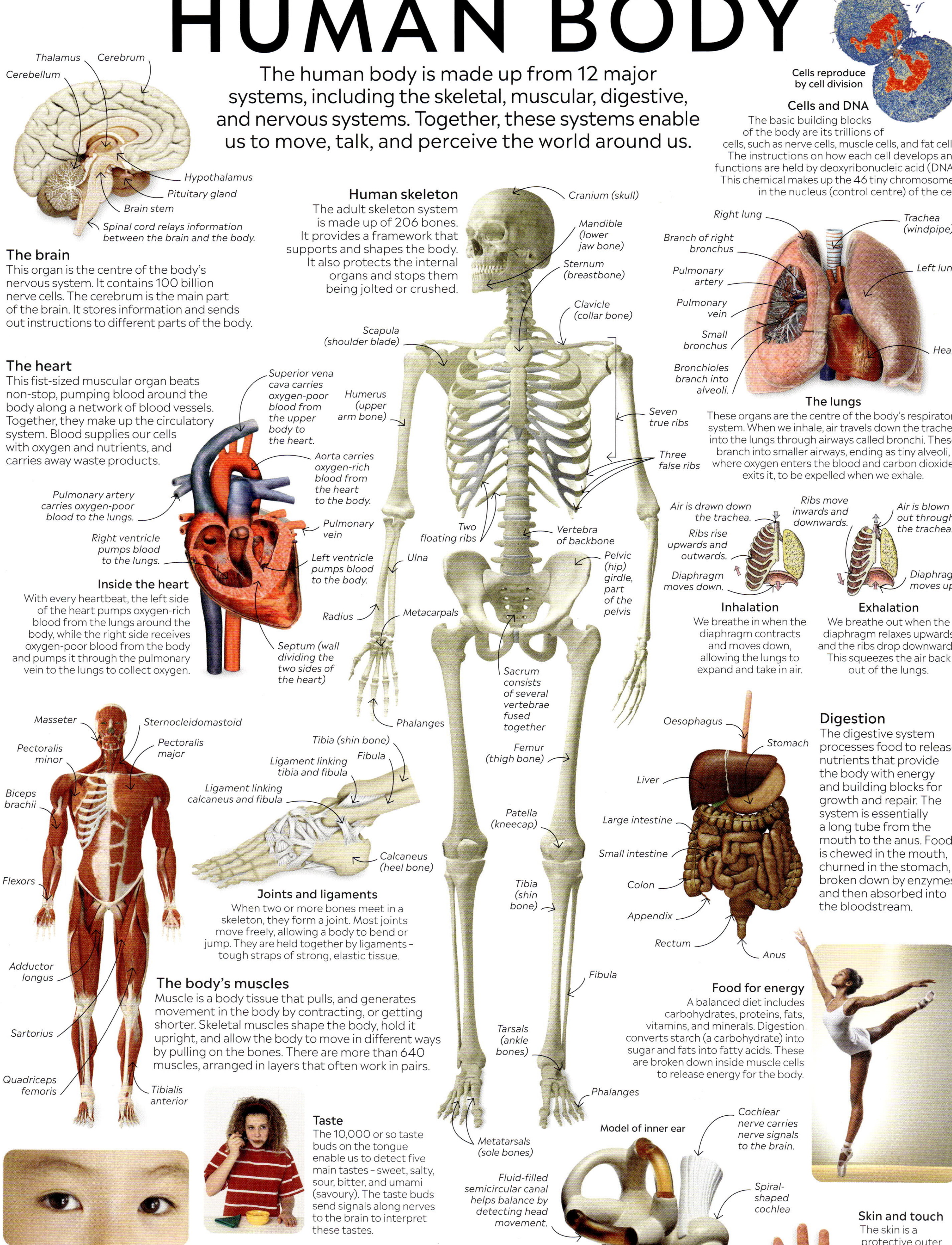

Cells and DNA
The basic building blocks of the body are its trillions of cells, such as nerve cells, muscle cells, and fat cells. The instructions on how each cell develops and functions are held by deoxyribonucleic acid (DNA). This chemical makes up the 46 tiny chromosomes in the nucleus (control centre) of the cell.

The brain
This organ is the centre of the body's nervous system. It contains 100 billion nerve cells. The cerebrum is the main part of the brain. It stores information and sends out instructions to different parts of the body.

Human skeleton
The adult skeleton system is made up of 206 bones. It provides a framework that supports and shapes the body. It also protects the internal organs and stops them being jolted or crushed.

The heart
This fist-sized muscular organ beats non-stop, pumping blood around the body along a network of blood vessels. Together, they make up the circulatory system. Blood supplies our cells with oxygen and nutrients, and carries away waste products.

Inside the heart
With every heartbeat, the left side of the heart pumps oxygen-rich blood from the lungs around the body, while the right side receives oxygen-poor blood from the body and pumps it through the pulmonary vein to the lungs to collect oxygen.

The lungs
These organs are the centre of the body's respiratory system. When we inhale, air travels down the trachea into the lungs through airways called bronchi. These branch into smaller airways, ending as tiny alveoli, where oxygen enters the blood and carbon dioxide exits it, to be expelled when we exhale.

Inhalation
We breathe in when the diaphragm contracts and moves down, allowing the lungs to expand and take in air.

Exhalation
We breathe out when the diaphragm relaxes upwards and the ribs drop downwards. This squeezes the air back out of the lungs.

Digestion
The digestive system processes food to release nutrients that provide the body with energy and building blocks for growth and repair. The system is essentially a long tube from the mouth to the anus. Food is chewed in the mouth, churned in the stomach, broken down by enzymes, and then absorbed into the bloodstream.

Joints and ligaments
When two or more bones meet in a skeleton, they form a joint. Most joints move freely, allowing a body to bend or jump. They are held together by ligaments – tough straps of strong, elastic tissue.

The body's muscles
Muscle is a body tissue that pulls, and generates movement in the body by contracting, or getting shorter. Skeletal muscles shape the body, hold it upright, and allow the body to move in different ways by pulling on the bones. There are more than 640 muscles, arranged in layers that often work in pairs.

Food for energy
A balanced diet includes carbohydrates, proteins, fats, vitamins, and minerals. Digestion converts starch (a carbohydrate) into sugar and fats into fatty acids. These are broken down inside muscle cells to release energy for the body.

Taste
The 10,000 or so taste buds on the tongue enable us to detect five main tastes – sweet, salty, sour, bitter, and umami (savoury). The taste buds send signals along nerves to the brain to interpret these tastes.

Senses
The body's senses include sight, hearing, touch, taste, and smell. The eyes contain more than 70 per cent of the body's sensory receptors. Hearing provides the brain with information that helps us work out the source, direction, and type of sounds.

Smell
Humans can distinguish billions of different odours. When stimulated by odour molecules, such as from a flower, sensory receptors in the nasal cavity send signals along nerves to the brain for processing.

Ears and hearing
Ears detect pressure waves that travel through the air from a source of sound. These sound waves cause the eardrum to vibrate. Tiny bones relay the vibrations to the inner ear, where sound receptors turn them into nerve signals. These signals are interpreted by the brain as sounds.

Skin and touch
The skin is a protective outer covering that defends the body from infection, controls water loss, and regulates the body's temperature. It also contains sensory receptors to detect touch, pressure, and temperature.

Japan's Tokaido Shinkansen "bullet" train passes by Mount Fuji

TRAIN

The first steam railways opened at the start of the 19th century. This new form of transport spread quickly across the world, heralding the age of the steam train. Steam power lasted until the mid-20th century, when it was replaced by diesel engines and electric motors.

Stagecoach travel

Before railways, the fastest means of travel was by stagecoach. By swapping teams of horses when they tired, stagecoaches could travel at an average speed of around 11 kph (7 mph).

Trevithick's train

The first working steam locomotive was built by British engineer Richard Trevithick in 1804. This engraving shows a locomotive he built in 1808.

Overcoming obstacles

As railway systems grew, engineers had to work out how to overcome natural obstacles, such as rivers or mountains. Gradually, engineering skills improved. Tunnels were carved through mountains, and bridges spanned deep valleys or gorges. Powerful locomotives were developed to haul trains up steep slopes.

Worker's pick

Building the railways

The first railways were built using picks, shovels, wheelbarrows, and wooden scaffolding. The route had to be as level as possible, so workers had to build embankments, make cuts or tunnels, and construct bridges. Early cuts were made with basic hand tools. Later, gunpowder was used to blast through solid rock.

Stephenson's *Rocket*

British engineer George Stephenson, known as the "father of railways", built the very first public railway in 1825. His son, Robert, built the famous locomotive *Rocket*.

Reproduction of Robert Stephenson's *Rocket*, 1829

The age of steam

By the end of the 19th century, steam trains were in use worldwide. They all had the same basic design. A coal fire heated up water in the train's boiler, producing steam that moved a piston back and forth. The movement of the piston turned the train's wheels. The crew included the driver and a fireman, who stoked the fire to maintain a constant supply of steam.

German steam engine, built in 1937

Number plate

Flanged wheel fits over plain-edge rail

Fish-belly rail, on stone sleepers

Fish-belly rails

Early cast-iron fish-belly rails were designed for extra strength. Each rail had a deeper section midway to strengthen it, but still broke easily under heavy weights. So engineers started using wrought-iron and, from the 1870s, longer-lasting steel rails.

Class travel

The first public passenger trains had three classes of accommodation. By the 1850s, the railways of Europe and the US were offering first-class passengers luxury facilities, including heating, lighting, toilets, and catering.

Dining cars

In 1865, American businessman George Pullman introduced the first luxury sleeping cars, and later, first-class dining cars. These made travelling by rail a stylish affair for wealthier passengers.

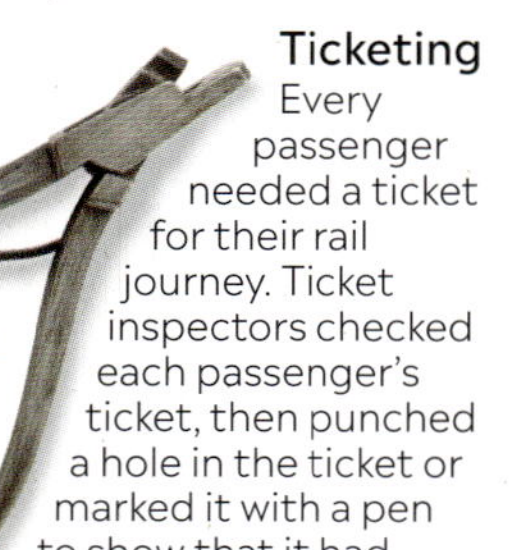

Ticket punch

Ticketing

Every passenger needed a ticket for their rail journey. Ticket inspectors checked each passenger's ticket, then punched a hole in the ticket or marked it with a pen to show that it had been inspected.

American first-class ticket

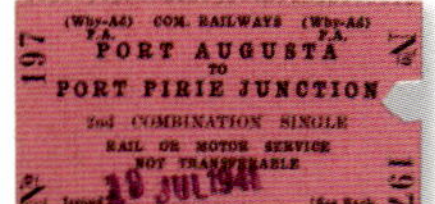

Australian second-class ticket

Diesel power

German engineer Rudolph Diesel demonstrated the first diesel engine in 1893, and built the world's first reliable diesel engine in 1897. In most diesel locomotives, such as this 1955 Deltic diesel-electric locomotive, the engine powers a generator, which produces an electric current. The current drives the electric motors that turn the wheels.

Liverpool Street station in London, UK

At the station

Stations in major towns or cities are often grand buildings. Large stations are designed to help thousands of travellers get on and off the trains quickly and easily. As trains use less fuel, carry more passengers and cargo, and produce less pollution than cars and trucks, many believe they are the best transport for the future.

Rapid transit trains

Electric rapid transit systems have been used successfully in airports in both the US and Europe. The driverless trains run on rubber tyres along a concrete track, guided by a central steel rail. All operations (such as speed, braking, and the opening and closing of doors) are controlled by a central computer.

Maglev trains

Instead of travelling on wheels along a rail, maglev (magnetic levitation) trains hover up to 15 mm (0.6 in) above a metal track and are pulled along by magnets.

21st-century speed

The Japanese Shinkansen, or "bullet" train, travels on specially built high-speed tracks at average speeds of 225 kph (140 mph). Other countries have designed tilting trains for high-speed travel on upgraded traditional lines.

Bullet train first ran in 1965.

A Lockheed SR-71 Blackbird aircraft

FLIGHT

For millennia, people longed to fly like birds, but it was only about 250 years ago that lighter-than-air balloons made flight a reality. In the 1900s, aeroplanes gave people greater freedom in the air. Now thousands of planes fly each day, enabling us to travel great distances with ease.

Pioneers of aviation

For centuries people have tried to fly, usually ending in disaster! But after 1800, Britain's George Cayley and Germany's Otto Lilienthal built working gliders. The age of powered flight began in 1903, with the Wright brothers' *Flyer* in the US.

Lilienthal's No.11 glider, 1895
Otto Lilienthal was the first to fly regularly and with control. He made about 2,000 glider flights.

Orville and Wilbur Wright's *Flyer* makes its first powered flight.

Lighter than air

Poster advertising airship travel

In 1783, the French Montgolfier brothers sent two men skyward in a hot-air balloon. Using hydrogen (a lighter-than-air gas) enabled longer trips, since hot-air flights ended when the air cooled. Later, propeller-driven, rigid-framed airships flew across the Atlantic, until a series of disasters caused by flammable hydrogen signalled their end.

De Havilland Tiger Moth cockpit, 1930s

Biplanes

Early biplanes (aircraft with two main wings stacked one above the other) were stronger but slower than the first monoplanes (aircraft with a single pair of wings).

Germany's LVG CVI, 1917

Flying gear, 1916

Flying gear

Warm clothing was vital for pilots in the cold and draughty open cockpits of early planes. This selection was issued to British pilots in World War I.

Spitfire
Built in 1938–1948 by Supermarine, this British fighter is a famous warplane.

Supermarine Spitfire

The evolving plane

Early monoplanes were structurally weak and accident-prone. In 1912, the French and British armies abandoned them for two-wing biplanes. By the mid-1920s, new techniques and materials made it possible to build stronger, more reliable monoplanes.

Flight controls

The basic flight control layout was set early on, with a joystick for pitching up and down, and rolling left and right, and a rudder bar at the pilot's feet.

Jet airliner flight deck
The flight deck of a modern jetliner has an array of electronic displays.

Anatomy of an aircraft

Launched in the US in 1933, the Boeing 247D was the first modern airliner. It had cantilever wings and a smooth all-metal skin. Its undercarriage retracted to minimize drag. These features, and its automatic pilot, are now standard. It carried 10 passengers; today's Airbus A380 (below) can hold more than 800.

Advanced airliner
The Boeing 247D was highly advanced. It could fly at 300 kph (180 mph), faster than most fighter planes.

Boeing 247D

Cierva C-30

Self-turning rotor
An autogyro is a craft whose spinning blades, which act as wings, are driven by the airflow up through the rotor.

Airbus 380
Built in response to the famous Boeing 747 "jumbo jet", the Airbus A380 is a giant of the skies. With a wingspan of 80 m (261 ft) it weighs around 575 tonnes on take-off.

The jet engine

Jet engines were invented in the late 1930s. They work by burning fuel, which pushes hot gas out at the back. The reaction, as it hits the air, thrusts the plane forwards. Most military planes, airliners, and small business planes use jet engines.

Rolls-Royce Tay turbofan engine

Helicopters

The highly manoeuvrable helicopter is the most versatile aircraft. The modern layout – a large main rotor and small tail rotor – was designed in 1939 by Igor Sikorsky. The Sikorsky R-4 (below) was the first mass-produced helicopter.

Sikorsky R-4, 1945

Balloons and airships

In the 1960s, new nylon balloons filled with hot air produced by burning propane gas sparked a revival in ballooning. Airships made a comeback in the 1980s, made from carbon fibre and plastics, and filled with safe helium rather than flammable hydrogen.

Hot-air balloon

Breaking the sound barrier
In 1947, US Air Force pilot Chuck Yeager broke the "sound barrier", flying the Bell X-1 faster than the speed of sound.

Bell X-1 rocket plane

Riding on air

The 1920s saw a renewed interest in gliders when people found that they could stay aloft for hours by riding rising bubbles of warm air, called thermals.

Zeppelin NT
In 1997, Zeppelin launched its New Technology (NT) craft. Holding two crew and 12 passengers, helium-filled NTs are much smaller than the Zeppelins of the 1930s.

F-35 Lightning II
Military aircraft are powerful machines. The Lockheed Martin F-35 Lightning II is designed to make it harder for enemy radar to detect.

Glider
With no engine, pure sailplanes are launched by winch or by being towed by a car or plane.

Hang-glider
Modern hang-gliders have highly efficient wing shapes, allowing them to use thermals to fly.

Schleicher ASK-13, 1966–present

Gold funerary mask of Pharaoh Tutankhamun

ANCIENT EGYPT

More than 5,000 years ago, the fertile Nile valley gave birth to the Egyptian civilization, which lasted more than 3,000 years. Ancient Egyptian rulers were called pharaohs and were believed to be descendants of the sun god, Re.

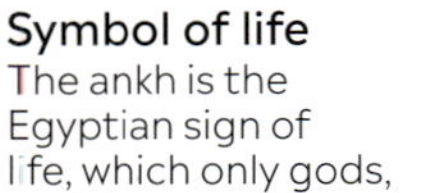

Symbol of life
The ankh is the Egyptian sign of life, which only gods, goddesses, and royalty were allowed to carry.

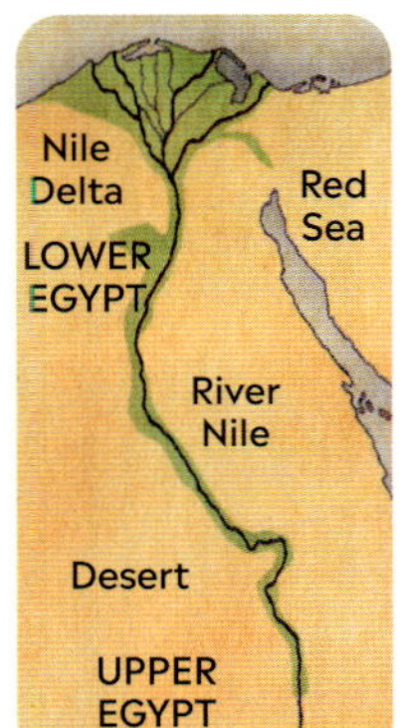

The Nile River
The Nile flooded every year, spreading rich silt on both its banks. This fertile area was called the "Black Land".

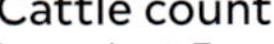

Cattle count
In ancient Egypt, a person's wealth was measured by the number of cattle they owned. This model shows officials counting cattle for tax records.

Farming by the Nile
The fertile land by the Nile enabled farmers to grow barley and wheat, as well as vegetables, such as beans and lentils.

Grapes

Dates

Pomegranate

Figs

Fruits
The ancient Egyptians grew grapes, dates, figs, and pomegranates. Grapes were used to make wine or for drying into raisins.

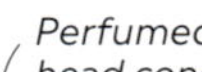

Musicians
Wall-paintings, songs on scrolls, and instruments found in tombs tell us that the ancient Egyptians enjoyed music. This group of musicians includes a woman playing a harp.

Perfumed head cone

Clothing
This woman is wearing a long dress of fine, pleated linen. Men wore shorter, wraparound kilts.

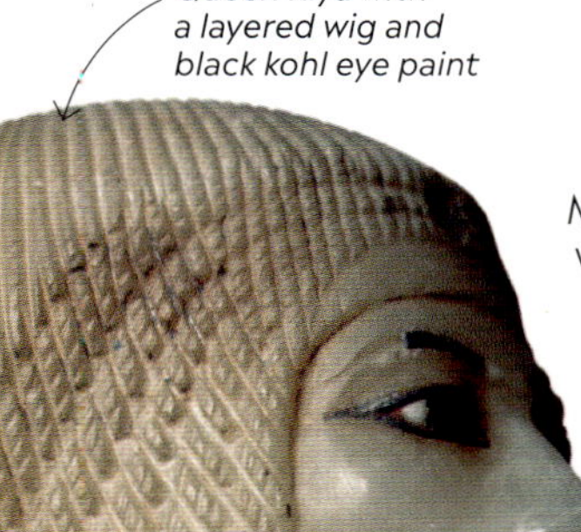

Queen Kiya with a layered wig and black kohl eye paint

Fashion and beauty
Egyptians used green and black eye paint. They often wore wigs and hair extensions made from human hair.

Famous mask
This mask made of gold and precious stones was found in 1922 in the tomb of the pharaoh Tutankhamun, who died in c.1324 BCE. The tomb contained many treasures as well as the pharaoh's mummified body.

Headdress

Collar

Outer coffin | Inner coffin | Mummy mask | Protective amulets | Linen bandages | Linen shroud | Embalmed body

Mummification
The ancient Egyptians believed that a dead person would need their body in the afterlife. So they preserved the body as a mummy to protect it from decay.

Mummified cat
Cats sacred to the goddess Bastet were mummified when they died. The mummies were wrapped in linen strips and had their faces painted.

Lucky charms
Made of gold and semi-precious stones, these lucky charms (amulets) were meant to bring the wearer good luck.

Fish amulets worn by young women

The god Heh symbolizes long life.

Beard of youth

Cowrie shells

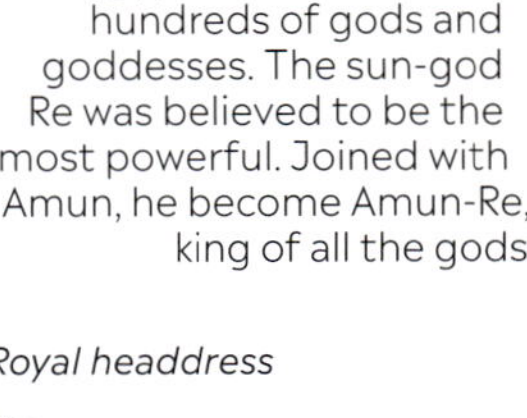

Sun disc set in the double feather crown

Amun-Re
The Egyptians worshipped hundreds of gods and goddesses. The sun-god Re was believed to be the most powerful. Joined with Amun, he become Amun-Re, king of all the gods.

Royal headdress

Female pharaoh
Nefertiti and her husband, Akhenaten, ruled Egypt jointly. In c.1350 BCE, they banned all gods except the sun-god Aten.

Papyrus
The Egyptians made paper from papyrus reeds that grew on the banks of the Nile.

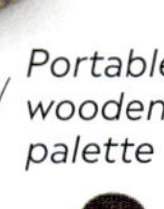

Portable wooden palette

Scribes
Scribes wrote with hieroglyphs, a form of picture-writing. They also used a faster script called hieratic, and later invented a third script called demotic.

Egyptian hieroglyphs

Rosetta Stone
Modern scholars could understand hieroglyphs only after the discovery of the Rosetta Stone in 1799. It included a Greek translation they could read.

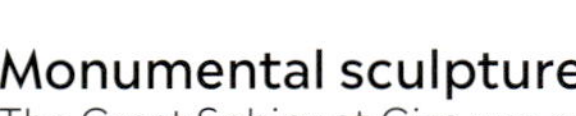

Monumental sculpture
The Great Sphinx at Giza was carved around 4,500 years ago to guard Pharaoh Khafre's pyramid. The sculpture has the ruler's head on a lion's body.

Inside a pyramid
Pyramids were built as burial places for kings and queens. This model is of the Great Pyramid at Giza, built for King Khufu by c.2500 BCE.

King's burial chamber

Temple for making offerings

Burial places of Khufu's female relatives

Gold funerary mask from c.16th century BCE, discovered in Mycenae, Greece

ANCIENT GREECE

The ancient Greek civilization flourished more than 2,500 years ago. From c.800 BCE, independent communities called city-states together produced a glorious culture in the arts, politics, architecture, and sport.

Carved capital supported the temple's roof.

Doric columns

The Parthenon
Athens' most impressive temple, the Parthenon, stands on the fortified citadel called the Acropolis.

Columns
In Greek architecture, the three main styles of column were the Doric, Ionic, and Corinthian.

Ionic

Doric

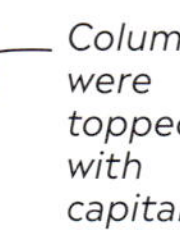

Corinthian

Columns were topped with capitals.

City-states
Each Greek city-state had a strong individual identity. At times, some of the city states joined together, to fight a mutual enemy.

Mycenaean Lion Gate
The Mycenaeans were great traders and warriors whose civilization flourished from c.1750 to 1120 BCE. The main entrance to their citadel at Mycenae was decorated with two stone lions.

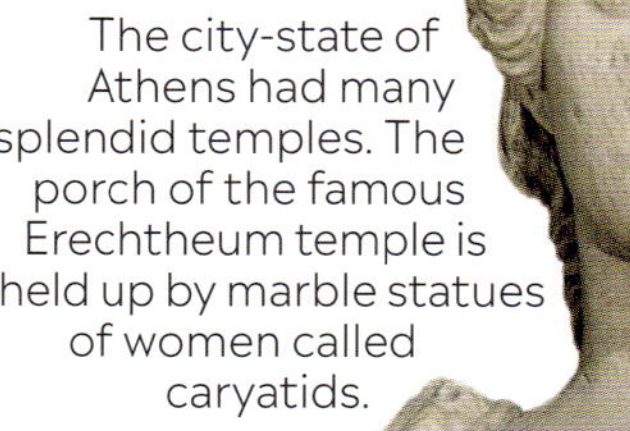

Athens
The city-state of Athens had many splendid temples. The porch of the famous Erechtheum temple is held up by marble statues of women called caryatids.

Caryatid may represent a priestess of the goddess Athena.

Dionysus, god of wine and fertility

Aphrodite, goddess of love and beauty

Poseidon, god of the sea

Hermes, messenger of the gods

Greek deities
The Greeks believed that their deities lived on Mount Olympus. Each one looked after a different area of life, such as love or war.

Greek vase, called an amphora

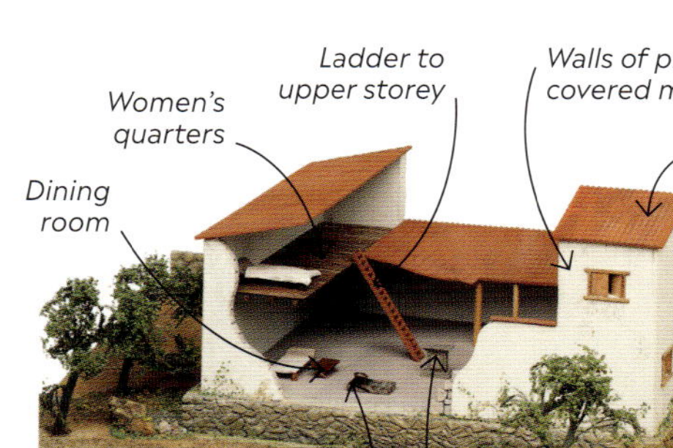

Women's quarters

Ladder to upper storey

Walls of plaster-covered mud bricks

Roof made of clay tiles

Dining room

Porch

Hearth, for cooking

Altar, for sacrifices to the gods

Stone foundations

Greek homes
Greek farmhouses were fairly simple, with walls made of dried mud bricks. Town houses were often more luxurious.

Men wore a tunic called a chiton.

Long chiton

Hair worn up and held in place with a net or ribbons

Family life
Men held all the power in Greek families. Women rarely took part in any form of public life. Only boys went to school. Girls helped at home and were married at the age of 12 or 13, usually to men chosen by their fathers.

Children wore the same clothes as adults.

Theatre at Epidaurus

Greek theatre
Greek theatres were built in a steep semi-circle to enable spectators at the back to see and hear the actors.

Statue of Aristotle

Philosophy
Aristotle (384–322 BCE) set up a school for philosophers in Athens called the Lyceum, where philosophy was taught through discussion.

Greek warships
Greek warships called triremes had pointed rams to sink enemy ships. They were rowed by 170 oarsmen who sat on three levels.

Ram

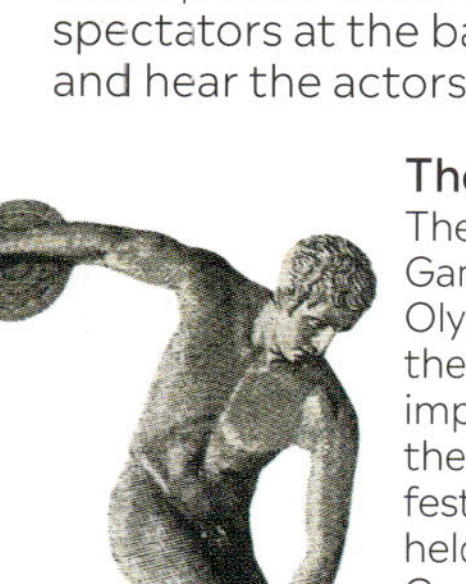

The games
The Olympic Games at Olympia were the most important of the athletic festivals held by the Greeks to honour the gods.

Greek athlete throwing a discus

Art and literature
Sappho, a poet who lived on the island of Lesbos, wrote about the lives of women.

Sappho, lyric poet, 7th century BCE

Alexander
Alexander the Great (356–323 BCE) was king of Macedonia. He created a vast empire and founded many new cities, such as Alexandria in Egypt.

The Colosseum in Rome, Italy

ANCIENT ROME

Rome began as a farming settlement on the banks of the River Tiber in Italy, around 1000 BCE. Over the next thousand years, it grew to become the capital of one of the greatest empires in history.

The founding of Rome
According to legend, Rome was founded by twins Romulus and Remus, who were raised by a she-wolf.

Republic and empire

Rome was a republic for 500 years, ruled by a Senate. Octavian became the first emperor in 27 BCE, and took the name *Imperator Caesar Augustus.*

Coin showing Emperor Augustus

The Roman army

The Roman army was known for its organization and discipline. It was made up of well-trained foot soldiers called legionaries. They were organized into small fighting units called centuries, which were grouped into cohorts and legions.

Helmet and crest
The helmet protected the head, face, and neck, without blocking the soldier's vision or hearing. Centurions and other officers wore crests on their helmets so their men could see them in battle.

Detachable crest

Neck protector

Cheek piece decorated with studs

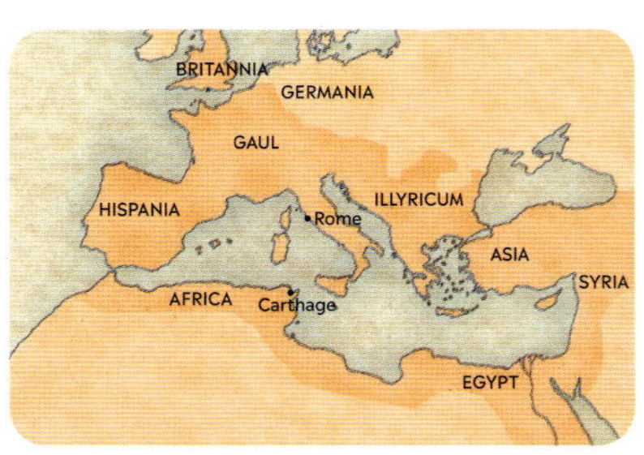

The Empire

By 117 CE, the Roman Empire included large parts of Europe, North Africa, and the Middle East. It was divided into provinces. Each province paid taxes to Rome, and its citizens were Roman subjects.

Overlapping shoulder plates

Ties and hooks hold the armour together.

Body armour
Roman body armour consisted of metal strips held together by leather straps on the inside. It was flexible but heavy, and soldiers had to help each other put it on and lace it up.

Red woollen tunic

Roman trading ship

Large square sails to catch the wind

Cargo hold

Pax Romana

In the 1st and 2nd centuries CE, there was a long period of peace called the *Pax Romana* (Roman Peace). Trade thrived, with merchants transporting goods across the Empire by ship or road.

Art and architecture

The Romans made fine pottery, delicate jewellery, and realistic sculptures. They were also skilled builders. Many of their theatres, bridges, and aqueducts are still standing today.

Violet-blue "core" glass

Figures carved from white glass

The Portland Vase
The Romans were highly skilled at glassmaking. This glass vessel was made by dipping a bubble of hot blue glass into molten white glass, then blowing the two layers together. When cool, the outer layer of white glass was cut away and carved.

Pont du Gard
The covered aqueduct on the upper level of this massive bridge carried up to 20,000 tonnes of fresh water from mountain springs to the city of Nîmes, France every day.

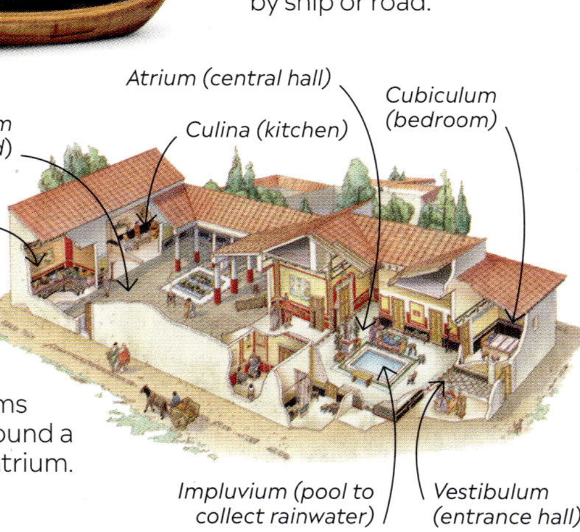

Town house

Wealthy Romans lived in a town house called a domus. The rooms were arranged around a hall called the atrium.

Citizen

Non-citizen

Enslaved person

Roman society
Romans were divided into three groups: citizens, non-citizens (people who came from outside Italy), and enslaved people. The richest citizens were nobles, called patricians. Most citizens were plebeians, or commoners. Only male citizens could wear the toga, a woollen robe draped over the shoulder and around the body.

Pilum
The pilum was a heavy javelin with a narrow point, designed to pierce shields and armour.

Sword and dagger
A soldier's main weapon was the gladius, a short stabbing sword. They also had a dagger called a pugio. Both were worn on the belt.

Dagger sheath

Iron hobnails on sole

Soldier's sandals
Military sandals (caligae) were as important as armour and weapons, because they had to survive miles of marching. The sandals were tough, flexible, and well ventilated.

Food in Roman Italy

Breakfast and lunch usually consisted of bread with honey, olives, and dates. Dinner was bread with a few vegetables, eggs, or spicy sausage. Only the wealthy had more elaborate dishes like the one shown here.

Songbirds with asparagus and quail eggs

End of the Empire

The Roman Empire was vast and hard to rule. It faced attacks from tribes in the north and the Persians in the east. In 395 CE, the Empire was split into two states, east and west. In 476 CE, the last western emperor lost power.

A B C D E F G
H I K L M N O P
Q R S T V X Y Z

Latin

Latin, the language of Rome, forms the basis of many modern European languages. The Latin alphabet had only 23 letters.

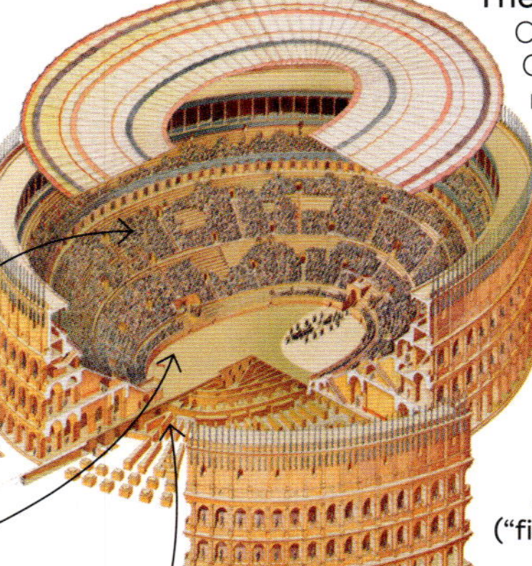

The Colosseum
Completed in 80 CE, the Colosseum was Rome's most famous amphitheatre. It had tiered seating for about 50,000 spectators. Giant canvas covers could be drawn across the top to shelter the crowd from the sun. Below the arena was a maze of underground chambers.

Tribes from the north
In the 5th century, northern tribes poured into the Empire. They founded many of the states of modern Europe. For example, the Franks turned Gaul into France.

Entertainment

Popular pastimes included playing board games or visiting a bathhouse. People also enjoyed watching plays and chariot races. The most popular spectator sports were fights involving gladiators and wild animals. Held in amphitheatres, these were often put on to mark a special event, such as a military victory, and could last several days.

Bathhouses
Most towns had public bathhouses where citizens would wash and meet friends. This well-preserved bathhouse is in the city of Bath in England.

Murmillo ("fish man")

Retiarius ("net man")

Gladiators
Gladiators were trained fighters who fought to the death. They were named after their costumes and weapons.

Eastern Empire
Emperor Constantine (right) founded the eastern capital city of Constantinople (Istanbul). The Eastern Empire (or Byzantine Empire) fell to the Ottoman Turks in 1453.

A Viking longship

VIKING

From the 8th to 11th centuries, Viking warriors and explorers sailed from Norway, Sweden, and Denmark to raid towns across Europe. They were excellent shipbuilders, traders, and metalworkers. Viking stories (sagas) are rich in gods, heroes, and epic battles.

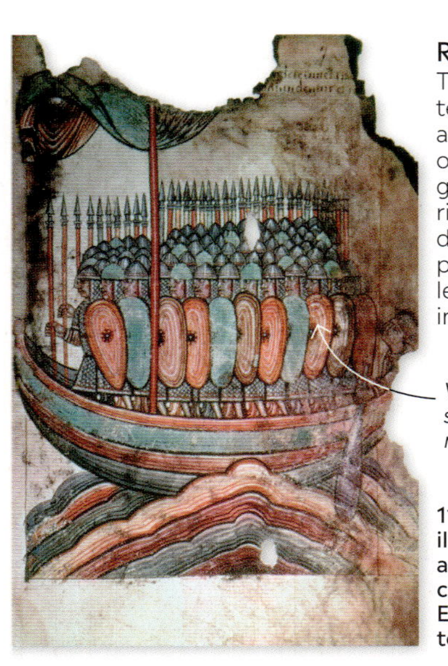

Viking warriors stand armed and ready to fight.

11th-century illustration of a Viking ship crossing the English Channel towards France

Raiding Europe

The Vikings terrorized towns along the coasts of western Europe, grabbing land and riches. They often demanded huge payments for leaving an area in peace.

Exploration

The Vikings were daring explorers. They sailed their ships into the frozen, uncharted waters of the North Atlantic Ocean, reaching as far as Greenland and North America.

Modern tapestry showing Leif the Lucky reaching North America around 1001 CE

Iron helmet from Norway

Spear

Padded leather tunic

Strap to carry a sword

Round wooden shield with a central iron boss

Tweed trousers

Woollen bindings

Reconstruction of Viking arms and armour

Armour

Viking lords may have given weapons and armour to their followers, but farmers serving in the army had to equip themselves. They used leather helmets and tunics, which were cheaper than iron helmets and mail.

Feared warriors

To a Viking warrior, honour and glory in battle were the only things that lasted. He had to be ready to follow his lord or king into battles or raids. Members of a loyal band of followers could be called up to fight at any moment.

Weapons

A warrior's most prized possessions were his spear, axe, shield, and sword. Weapons were made of iron, often inlaid with silver or copper. Warriors were usually buried with their weapons.

Superb sailors

The Vikings built ships and boats of many shapes and sizes for different uses. The longest, fastest ships were designed for raiding. There were also fishing boats, passenger ferries, and small boats for travelling on lakes.

Anchor made of wood and stone

Quern stone for grinding grain into flour

Farming

Living in the far north, Viking farmers often had to work infertile land in harsh weather. They grew barley, rye, and spelt, an early form of wheat. They also raised sheep, cows, pigs, goats, horses, poultry, and geese.

Viking women

While the men were away, women ran the farms, and a few may even have been warriors. Most spent part of the day spinning and weaving.

Woman spinning wool into yarn

Spun wool on spindle

Toy sword

Toy spear

Growing up

Viking children did not go to school. They worked in the fields and helped in the home. Viking boys played with toy weapons. They began weapon practice in their teens.

Viking gods

The Vikings believed in many deities. Chief among them were Odin, god of wisdom and war, Thor, the defender of the gods, and Frey, the god of fertility.

Beard was a symbol of growth.

Statuette of Frey

Frey and Freyja

People called on Frey for rich crops, and to bless them with children. Frey's sister Freyja was a goddess of fertility and love.

Thor's hammer

Thor was popular with peasants and farmers. He killed evil monsters with his mighty hammer.

Silver Thor's hammer pendant

A Valkyrie welcoming the hero

Curved roof of Valhalla

Hero on horseback

Warriors on Viking ship

Tjängvide Stone from Gotland, Sweden

Picture of Valhalla

Valkyries were mythical warrior women who searched battlefields for slain warriors and took them to Valhalla, the "hall of the dead". On this picture stone, a hero arrives at Valhalla on Odin's eight-legged horse.

Funeral pyres

Some funeral ships were not buried, but set alight in a blazing pyre, as in this re-enactment.

Death and burial

Vikings were buried with everything they would need in the afterlife. The wealthy were buried in ships to carry them to the next world, along with their clothes, weapons, and furniture. The funeral ship was covered with a mound of earth.

Carved prow

Oseberg ship

This ship was found in a burial mound in Oseberg, Norway, in 1903. It was probably the funeral ship of a 9th-century queen.

Silver cloak pin from Denmark

Twisted gold wire

Gold brooch from Denmark

Jewellery

The Vikings loved jewellery. Surviving examples include necklaces, arm-rings (like bracelets), brooches, and finger-rings.

Arm-rings

Some arm-rings were spiral in shape. This one is a flattened gold band with fine decoration.

Cross

Tree

Gold arm-ring from Denmark

Keyholders

Keys were symbols of responsibility. Women were in charge of the locked chest that held family valuables.

9th-century bronze key from Denmark

Christ with outstretched arms as if on a cross

Modern copy of the Jelling Stone

End of the Viking age

In the late 10th century, Viking kings began to convert to Christianity to strengthen their power. By the 12th century, they ceased raiding and slowly disappeared from history. Carved in Denmark in about 965 CE, the Jelling Stone bears the oldest picture of Jesus Christ in Scandinavia.

A re-enactment of medieval combat

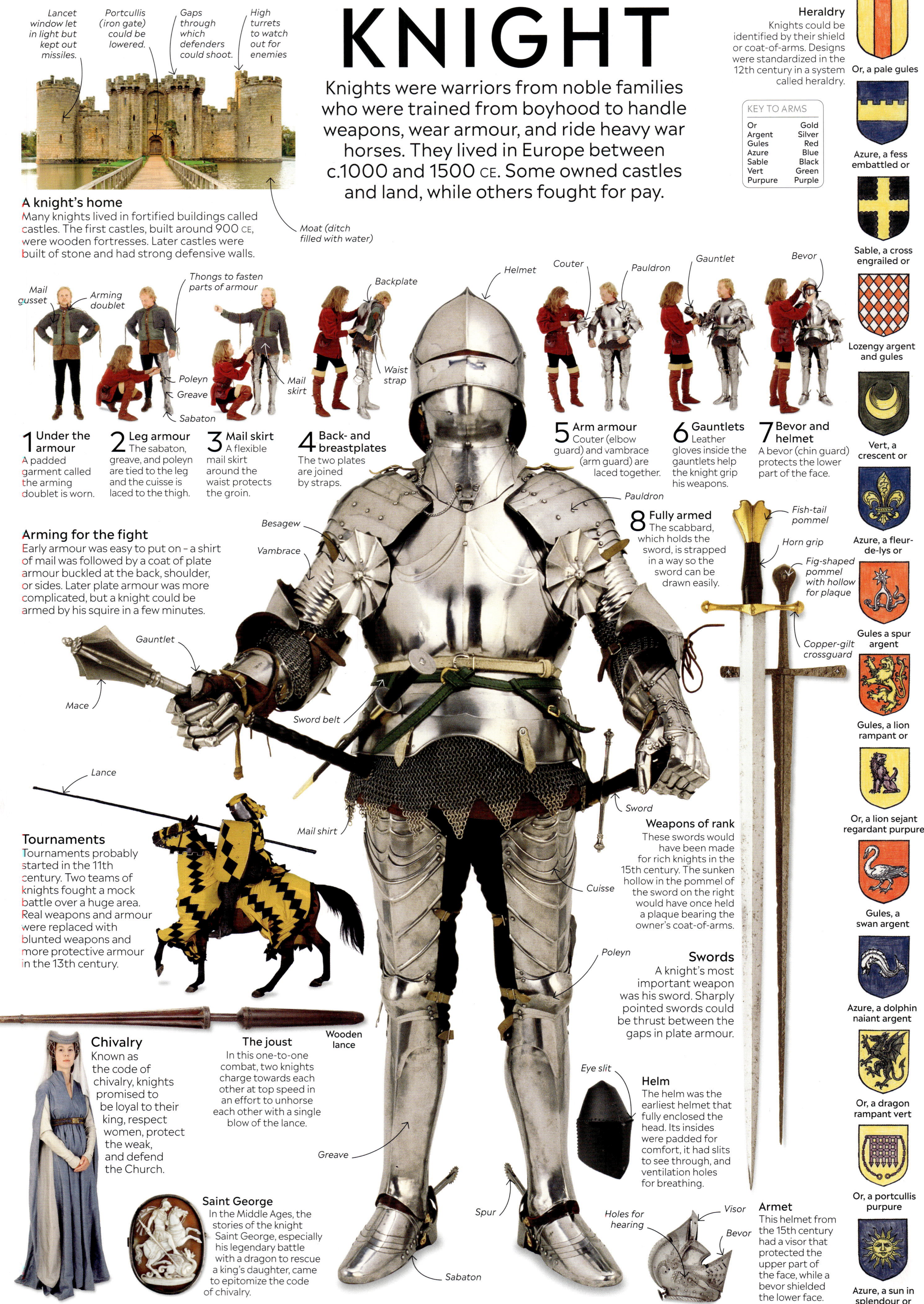
KNIGHT
Knights were warriors from noble families who were trained from boyhood to handle weapons, wear armour, and ride heavy war horses. They lived in Europe between c.1000 and 1500 CE. Some owned castles and land, while others fought for pay.
Lancet window let in light but kept out missiles.
Portcullis (iron gate) could be lowered.
Gaps through which defenders could shoot.
High turrets to watch out for enemies
Moat (ditch filled with water)
A knight's home
Many knights lived in fortified buildings called castles. The first castles, built around 900 CE, were wooden fortresses. Later castles were built of stone and had strong defensive walls.
Heraldry
Knights could be identified by their shield or coat-of-arms. Designs were standardized in the 12th century in a system called heraldry.
KEY TO ARMS
Or Gold
Argent Silver
Gules Red
Azure Blue
Sable Black
Vert Green
Purpure Purple
Or, a pale gules
Azure, a fess embattled or
Sable, a cross engrailed or
Lozengy argent and gules
Vert, a crescent or
Azure, a fleur-de-lys or
Gules a spur argent
Gules, a lion rampant or
Or, a lion sejant regardant purpure
Gules, a swan argent
Azure, a dolphin naiant argent
Or, a dragon rampant vert
Or, a portcullis purpure
Azure, a sun in splendour or
Mail gusset
Arming doublet
Thongs to fasten parts of armour
Poleyn
Greave
Sabaton
Mail skirt
Backplate
Waist strap
Helmet
Couter
Pauldron
Gauntlet
Bevor
1 Under the armour
A padded garment called the arming doublet is worn.
2 Leg armour
The sabaton, greave, and poleyn are tied to the leg and the cuisse is laced to the thigh.
3 Mail skirt
A flexible mail skirt around the waist protects the groin.
4 Back- and breastplates
The two plates are joined by straps.
5 Arm armour
Couter (elbow guard) and vambrace (arm guard) are laced together.
6 Gauntlets
Leather gloves inside the gauntlets help the knight grip his weapons.
7 Bevor and helmet
A bevor (chin guard) protects the lower part of the face.
Arming for the fight
Early armour was easy to put on – a shirt of mail was followed by a coat of plate armour buckled at the back, shoulder, or sides. Later plate armour was more complicated, but a knight could be armed by his squire in a few minutes.
Besagew
Vambrace
Pauldron
8 Fully armed
The scabbard, which holds the sword, is strapped in a way so the sword can be drawn easily.
Fish-tail pommel
Horn grip
Fig-shaped pommel with hollow for plaque
Copper-gilt crossguard
Gauntlet
Mace
Sword belt
Lance
Sword
Mail shirt
Weapons of rank
These swords would have been made for rich knights in the 15th century. The sunken hollow in the pommel of the sword on the right would have once held a plaque bearing the owner's coat-of-arms.
Tournaments
Tournaments probably started in the 11th century. Two teams of knights fought a mock battle over a huge area. Real weapons and armour were replaced with blunted weapons and more protective armour in the 13th century.
Cuisse
Poleyn
Swords
A knight's most important weapon was his sword. Sharply pointed swords could be thrust between the gaps in plate armour.
Wooden lance
Chivalry
Known as the code of chivalry, knights promised to be loyal to their king, respect women, protect the weak, and defend the Church.
The joust
In this one-to-one combat, two knights charge towards each other at top speed in an effort to unhorse each other with a single blow of the lance.
Eye slit
Helm
The helm was the earliest helmet that fully enclosed the head. Its insides were padded for comfort, it had slits to see through, and ventilation holes for breathing.
Greave
Saint George
In the Middle Ages, the stories of the knight Saint George, especially his legendary battle with a dragon to rescue a king's daughter, came to epitomize the code of chivalry.
Spur
Sabaton
Holes for hearing
Visor
Bevor
Armet
This helmet from the 15th century had a visor that protected the upper part of the face, while a bevor shielded the lower face.

A 1912 travel poster promoting the *Titanic*

TITANIC

The grand passenger ship RMS *Titanic* was claimed to be "virtually unsinkable". The sinking of the vessel with huge loss of life on its maiden voyage has fascinated millions, and inspired countless films, books, and musicals.

White Star Line

The White Star Line, which built the *Titanic*, was founded in 1871 by Liverpool ship-owner Thomas Ismay. The line was bought by US banker, industrialist, and railroad owner John Pierpont Morgan in 1903.

WHITE STAR LINE

ATLANTIC OCEAN

New York

Titanic wreck site

Queenstown

Southampton

Cherbourg

Disaster strikes

The *Titanic* sailed from Southampton, UK, on 10 April 1912, stopping at Cherbourg, France, and Queenstown, Ireland, before setting out across the North Atlantic for New York, US. It received several ice warnings from other ships, but continued to sail at full speed. When a lookout spotted an iceberg at 11:40 pm on 14 April, it was too late to avoid a collision.

Destination New York City

Many of the passengers on the *Titanic* were leaving behind poverty in Europe to start a new life in the Americas. Between 1900 and 1914, more than 12 million people emigrated by travelling steerage (third-class) on North Atlantic liners.

Statue of Liberty, New York, US

On the bridge

Captain Edward Smith and his officers commanded the ship from the bridge on the boat deck. The captain steered the ship from the wheelhouse, just behind the bridge. Inside the hull, firemen and stokers shovelled coal into the boilers to keep the engines working at full speed.

Funnel

Crow's-nest (for lookout)

Forecastle deck

Bridge

Boat deck (topmost of 10 decks)

A deck (with promenade)

B deck (bridge deck)

C deck (first-class suites)

D deck (first-class saloon)

E deck (upper deck)

F deck (middle deck)

G deck (lower deck)

Waterline

Orlop deck and tank top house engines and boilers.

Model of the Titanic

How the *Titanic* sank

The *Titanic* struck the iceberg on the starboard (right) side of its hull. The iceberg punched a series of holes along the hull, which started to flood with seawater. Those lucky enough to get a place on a lifeboat watched in horror as the ship sank beneath the waves.

Stage 1

One by one the ship's "watertight" compartments filled with water. The bow (front) slowly sank under the weight, pulling the stern (rear) out of the water. This put a great strain on the keel (the bottom running along the length of the ship).

Stage 2

The weight of water inside the hull pulled the ship's bow under. The stern lifted in the air, causing funnels, engines, and internal fittings to break loose.

Stage 3

The strain on the keel made it fracture. This caused the stern section to right itself temporarily, and float upright in the water for a few minutes.

Stage 4

The ship's bow plummeted about 3,800 m (12,500 ft) to the ocean floor, breaking free of the stern. The stern floated by itself momentarily before it, too, sank below the waves at 2:20 am.

On-board luxury

First-class passengers had spacious staterooms (cabins), promenade decks, and dining rooms. Second-class passengers also travelled in comfort. Even those travelling third-class enjoyed running water and table linen – many for the first time in their lives.

The grand staircase led from the first-class dining saloon to the first-class promenade deck.

Giant of the sea

Built in Belfast, Northern Ireland in 1909–1912, the *Titanic* could carry up to 3,547 people and was the biggest ship of her day. From the stern to the bow, she stretched 269 m (882 ft 9 in).

Backstay to hold up rear mast

Rear ventilation funnel

Lifeboat (one of 20 – enough for only half the people on board)

Promenade deck for the first-class.

Officers' quarters on boat deck

Foremast

Forestay to hold up foremast

Forestay fitting on bow

The bridge

Docking bridge for when the ship is in port

Rear mast

Poop deck for the third-class

Second-class entrance to boat deck

Cast-steel rudder

Double-bottomed hull

Keel

Loss of life

More than 1,500 people lost their lives on the *Titanic*. Newspapers had stories of the victims and the 706 survivors.

The death toll

The chart below shows how the death toll varied among the classes and crew.

First class

Deaths included 11 women and children and 119 men.

Second class

Deaths included 24 women and children and 142 men.

Third class

Deaths included 119 women and children and 417 men.

Crew

The death toll included three women and 682 men.

	Saved	Lost
First class	199	130
Second class	119	166
Third class	174	536
Crew	214	685

The search for the *Titanic*

The wreck of the *Titanic* was discovered in 1985. In 1987, scientists investigated the wreck further. They explored the seabed in a submersible (right).

Titanium sphere protected the crew from water pressure.

Submersible is 8 m (26 ft 6 in) long.

NAUTILE

Cameras and lights

Robotic arm

Raising the *Titanic*

Some people think the ship and its contents should be salvaged and put on display. But the cost would be huge, and some believe that taking items from the site is like robbing a grave.

A British Mark V tank with a cutaway section showing the inside

WORLD WAR I

Between 1914 and 1918, the world was engulfed in a war of a ferocity and scale never seen before, with people from every continent taking part in the fighting. By the time the war ended, the old empires were in ruins and around 10 million soldiers had lost their lives.

In the trenches
In western Europe, the opposing armies dug trenches to defend their positions and troops from enemy fire.

The German Army
By 1914, Germany had the strongest army in Europe, with 840,000 men and more than three million reserves. It fought alongside Turkey, Bulgaria, and Austria-Hungary.

Steel helmet

Mauser rifle

German soldier, 1916–1917

The British Army
In 1914, Britain had 247,432 regular soldiers and 218,280 reservists. The Allied armies of Britain, France, and Russia were joined by six other nations and the US.

Short Magazine Lee Enfield Mark III rifle

British soldier in winter uniform, 1914–1915

British basic kit
To fight and survive in the trenches, a British soldier's kit included a rifle and bayonet, ammunition, an entrenching tool to dig holes for cover, latrines, and graves, and, by 1917, a respirator in case of poison gas attacks.

Goggles to protect eyes from corrosive gas

Respirator gas mask with air tube

Water bottle

Entrenching tool handle

Bayonet

Aerial warfare
The first warplanes flew over enemy lines on reconnaissance missions. Soon, fighter planes were firing on each other in dogfights in the sky. The most famous pilot of the war was German airman Manfred von Richthofen (1892–1918), known as the Red Baron because of his red Fokker plane (below).

Symbol of the German airforce

Barrel

Pivot changes direction and angle of the gun.

U-boat gun
German U-boats operated under the sea and sank around 5,550 Allied and neutral merchant ships and as many warships.

Stock *Telescopic sight* *Barrel* *Trigger*

Sniper's rifle
Trained marksmen called snipers had rifles fitted with telescopic sights, which fired accurately at longer ranges.

German MG 08 Maxim machine gun

Machine guns
Machine guns fired up to 600 bullets a minute. They were small, highly effective, and difficult to destroy.

British Mills bomb

German stick grenade

French trench knife

German trench club

Close-combat weapons
Soldiers carried close-combat weapons in case they had to kill an enemy silently or in a tight space. Hand-thrown grenades were used to clear fortified enemy positions.

Pigeon carrier basket

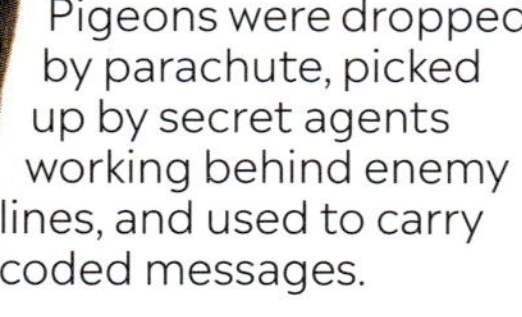

Pigeon post
Pigeons were dropped by parachute, picked up by secret agents working behind enemy lines, and used to carry coded messages.

Horse-drawn ambulance

Emergency transport
Both sides had a fleet of field ambulances to transport the wounded.

Wire cutters
Advancing troops had to cut rows of barbed-wire that protected the trenches and "no-man's land" in between.

German wire cutters

Artillery
Light field artillery guns were pulled by horses, and heavier guns by tractor. Their bombardment could destroy trenches, artillery, and communications.

German 7.7 cm FK 96 n.A. field gun

Saws and knives for amputation

Surgeon's kit
Army doctors carried a standard set of surgical instruments. They treated a wide range of injuries from bullets and shell fragments.

Spoon *Fork* *Razor* *Razor case* *Button stick* *Knife* *Shaving brush* *Spare boot laces*

Soldier's small kit
A soldier's small kit contained personal items for everyday use.

Tank warfare
The British-invented tank played a vital role in the Allied advances of 1918 – flattening barbed-wire, crossing enemy trenches, and shielding advancing troops.

Driver's visor *Armour plating* *Machine-gun port* *Caterpillar track* *Side gun*

British Mark V tank

Treaty of Versailles
The war ended in 1918 when the Allies finally broke through the German lines. The peace treaty was signed on 28 June 1919 in the Palace of Versailles in France.

Victoria Cross (Britain) | Order of Osmanieh (Turkey) | *Légion d'Honneur* (France)

Medals of valour
Nations awarded medals to honour bravery.

The cost of war
Around 10 million soldiers and at least 6 million civilians died in the war. Poppies, which grew on the battlefields of Belgium, became the symbol of those killed.

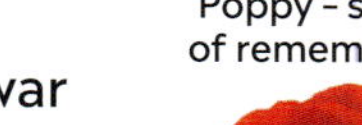

One of many war cemeteries in France

Poppy - symbol of remembrance

Into battle
Scrambling out of a trench into no-man's land between opposing lines was horrific. Armed with only rifles and bayonets, troops faced artillery bombardment and machine-gun fire.

A World War II Supermarine Spitfire Mk IX MH434 combat aircraft

WORLD WAR II

The war began in 1939 when Germany invaded Poland. In response, Britain and France declared war on Germany. By the end of the war in 1945, most nations had become involved and more than 60 million people had been killed.

Hitler and the Nazis

Adolf Hitler, leader of the Nazi Party, came to power in Germany in 1933 and set out to restore German power in Europe.

Protecting citizens

The British made plans to evacuate city children to the countryside, issued gas masks, and encouraged people to dig shelters for use in bombing raids.

Child's gas mask

War in the air

The Germans overpowered Europe in 1939–1940 with *Blitzkrieg* ("lightning war") tactics - using tank divisions or aerial bombing to open the way for ground troops. British planes fought back, ending the planned German invasion of Britain.

Spitfire MkV

Three-bladed propeller

Streamlined nose

1,470 horsepower liquid-cooled engine

Rear-view mirror

Cockpit

Symbol of the Royal Air Force (RAF)

Metal rear fuselage

Retractable landing gear (undercarriage)

British Royal Air Force (RAF) planes

The RAF's Spitfire Mk 1A, with speeds up to 582 kph (362 mph), was faster at high altitudes and more manoeuvrable than the German Messerschmitt Bf109E. From 1941, the RAF used the Spitfire MkV, which had a more powerful engine.

British soldier, American soldier, Soviet soldier, Italian soldier, German soldier, Japanese soldier, Australian soldier

Allies and Axis powers

The Allies included Britain, Australia, South Africa, Canada, French and Polish exiles, and, from 1941, the USSR and the US. The Axis was Germany, Italy, and Japan, and later, Hungary, Romania, Bulgaria, Croatia, and Slovakia.

Messerschmitt Bf109E

Radio transmitter

Single-seat cockpit

Nazi symbol

German Air Force (Luftwaffe) planes

The German Messerschmitt Bf109E had a 1,150-horsepower engine, and was armed with four machine guns and one cannon. The Stuka was used in the *Blitzkrieg* to dive out of the sky and drop bombs.

White paint for winter camouflage

Soviet T-34 tank

Tank warfare

Heavily armoured tanks were used on all fronts. The Soviet T-34 was the most produced tank during the war.

76-mm gun

Swivelling gun turret

Caterpillar tracks

US M4 Sherman tank

USS *Alabama* battleship

War at sea

German U-boats (submarines) and destroyers attacked Allied supply ships in the North Atlantic. The US Navy also battled Japanese forces in the Pacific Ocean. The USS *Alabama* served in the Atlantic and the Pacific.

Boeing B-17 Flying Fortress

The Blitz

German planes bombed British cities from the air, which the British called the "Blitz", short for *Blitzkrieg.*

US Army Air Force (USAAF)

The USAAF's Boeing B-17 Flying Fortress carried out high-altitude daylight bombings against German forces.

Plexiglass nose for the bombadier, who operated a bombsight, containing bomb release switches

Ball turret with twin guns

Remote-controlled chin turret

Main undercarriage retracts rearwards

Wingspan of 31.6 m (103.7 ft)

Biber submarine

Periscope

Viewing port

Warhead

Propeller

Torpedo

Submarines

Germany's large fleet of U-boats hunted Allied ships, and their one-man submarines (Bibers) damaged Allied supply ships near northern France and the Netherlands in 1944–1945.

Japanese prayer flag

All Japanese servicemen carried prayer flags into battle. Relatives wrote prayers and blessings on the Japanese flag's background.

Pearl Harbor

On 7 December 1941, Japanese planes attacked the US Pacific Fleet at Pearl Harbor in Hawaii. The following day, the US declared war on Japan and Germany.

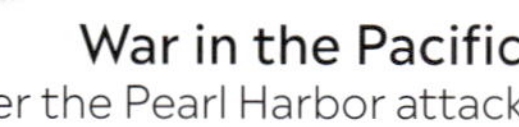

War in the Pacific

After the Pearl Harbor attack, Japan advanced across Southeast Asia and the Pacific. In 1942, the US Navy defeated the Japanese at two Pacific battles, halting Japan's advance.

Aerial photograph of French coastline

D-Day landings

On 6 June 1944 (D-Day), US, British, and Canadian troops landed on the coast of German-occupied France and advanced through Europe. In April 1945, the Soviets entered Berlin. Germany surrendered the following month. The end of the war in Europe, on 8 May, came to be known as VE (Victory in Europe) Day. Japan carried on fighting until 15 August 1945.

The Holocaust

The Holocaust ("sacrifice by burning") was the Nazi attempt to kill all Jewish people. Many Holocaust memorials are shaped like a *menorah* (Hebrew for candlestick).

Secret agent's pen-pistol

Firing button

End unscrewed to load 6.35-mm cartridge

Spying and secrets

Brave individuals spied on invading forces to sabotage enemy plans.

Enigma machine

This German machine sent coded messages, which were deciphered by European code-breakers, giving the Allies key information.

The Soviet Front

On 22 June 1941, 150 German divisions invaded the USSR. The Soviets resisted; the Germans were unable to capture key cities and were pushed back.

Memorial showing troops hoisting the US flag on the Pacific island of Iwo Jima

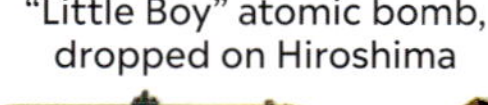

"Little Boy" atomic bomb, dropped on Hiroshima

Atomic bomb

On 6 August 1945, the US dropped an atomic bomb on Hiroshima in Japan, and on Nagasaki on the 9th.

United Nations (UN)

The UN was founded in 1945 to bring nations together and keep peace.